TO:

FROM:

DATE:

from where I stand

30 DAYS IN THE LIFE OF PAUL

Shanna Noel
with Sherri Gragg

INTRODUCTION

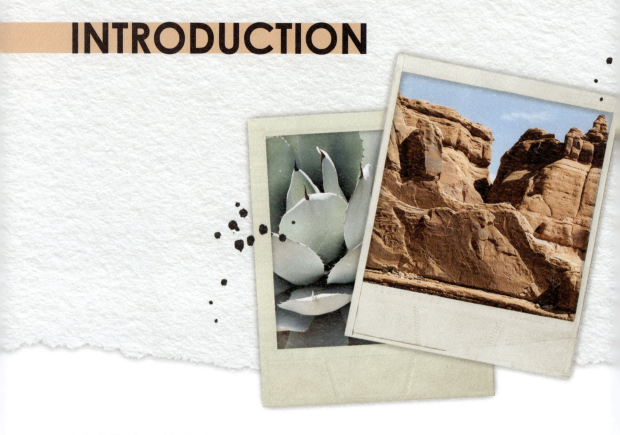

It is difficult to think of a man or woman in Scripture who provoked more powerful reactions than Paul. When Paul came to town, stones flew, whips cracked, and riots ignited.

But he was also well-loved. Scripture tells us that when he said his final goodbyes to the Ephesian elders, "They all wept as they embraced him and kissed him. What grieved them most was his statement that they would never see his face again" (Acts 20:37–38).

Today, more than two thousand years later, we also find ourselves experiencing strong, and often conflicting, emotions as we follow his story from Tarsus to Rome.

We are frustrated by his complex arguments and exasperated by his unwillingness to sugarcoat his opinions. Our hearts are at once touched by his tender love for the church and deeply saddened by the wounds he inflicts when his fiery temper rages out of control.

Love him or despise him, one truth is beyond debate: Paul was devoted to the one true God. Paul's deep and burning desire to remain faithful to God is the thread that weaves throughout the tapestry of his life without breaking. This unwavering devotion to God was Paul's inheritance, passed down from a long line of faithful men and women, finding its ultimate fulfillment in Jesus the Messiah.

Born into a devout Jewish family living in the Roman city of Tarsus, Paul was the product of two very different worlds. As the son of a Pharisee, the stories of his ancestors, prayer, and the study of God's law were the very air he breathed as his parents followed God's admonishment to ensure their children knew and obeyed His law.

"These commandments that I give you today are to be on your hearts. Impress them on your children. Talk about them when you sit at home and when you walk along the road, when you lie down and when you get up. Tie them as symbols on your hands and bind them on your foreheads" (Deuteronomy 6:6–8).

Born in the great city of Tarsus, he was also a Roman citizen. Outside the walls of his home and the synagogue, Roman culture, and the worship of a host of Roman "gods," colored every facet of life.

It is this unique upbringing, combined with a brilliant mind, that perfectly molded him into God's messenger of redemption to the Gentiles.

As we take this journey together, may we hold all these truths in tension, remembering that Paul was more than a character in Scripture, easily defined, categorized, and put in a box. Though undeniably extraordinary, he was still just a man—a flawed human being who sought after God with relentless devotion, stumbling, and growing, along the way.

May we find ourselves inspired and challenged by his love for God, while holding his weaknesses and failings in the tender grace he so loved, and in doing so, perhaps learn to offer that same grace more fully to ourselves and others.

**"For it is by grace you have been saved, through faith—
and this is not from yourselves, it is the gift of God—
not by works, so that no one can boast."**

EPHESIANS 2:8–9

CONTENTS

DAY 1

Tarsus

Breathe in. Breathe out.

A young Jewish woman sits on the birthing stool, gripping the handles on each side of her until her knuckles turn white. One midwife stands behind her, arms wrapped around her upper torso, supporting her. The other kneels at her feet, hands poised to receive new life into the world.

The child's father, a devout Pharisee, prays as he paces anxiously back and forth across the courtyard of the home.

On the other side of the courtyard wall, the streets of Tarsus are a hive of activity. Gold flows freely as merchants traveling the Roman road between Cilicia and Syria trade their wares. Men laugh and chat as they enter the public baths, while some of the greatest philosophical minds in history debate ethics nearby.

But on this day, tucked away in a quiet home of a Jewish tentmaker, none of the splendor of Tarsus matters. Here, as a mother labors, life has narrowed to one small point.

Breathe in. Breathe out. Knuckles white on the handles of the birthing stool.

Be brave now. Be strong. You are almost there.

And with one last cry, a baby boy is born.

From birth, the child is equally a citizen of Rome and a descendant of Abraham. His bright mind will be shaped by both Roman philosophers and his father's careful instruction in the Torah. He is the needle point of convergence between the pagan Roman Empire and God's covenant people.

After a quiet moment with his mother, the baby is swaddled and taken to meet his father.

When the midwives place the screaming bundle into his calloused hands, the new father smiles joyfully and names his son Saul, although the boy will be called Paul by his Roman neighbors.

Then, as the new father's eyes fill with tears, he recites the Shema over his son for the first time.

"Hear, O Israel: The Lord our God, the Lord is one" (Deuteronomy 6:4 NIV).

It is a prayer of faithful devotion—a steadfast declaration that God's chosen people will remain faithful to the one true God. The prayer will ring in young Saul's ears as he runs in play, and as he pushes needle through leather as a tentmaker's apprentice.

The Shema will echo with Saul's footsteps along Roman cobblestones and follow him to Jerusalem when he leaves home to study under the famous rabbi Gamliel.

This prayer of faithful devotion—the one his father spoke over him as a newborn—will remain constant in Saul's mind and heart always, even when Jesus of Nazareth turns his world upside down.

The Shema will sustain him, comfort him, and strengthen him as he answers the Messiah's call, and in doing so, changes the world.

He was born into this exact time and place for this holy purpose, but for now, the newborn quiets, yawns, and drifts off to sleep to the sound of his father's prayers.

"The Lord our God, the Lord is one . . ."

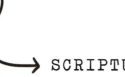

SCRIPTURE READING

Saul's upbringing as a devout Jew was firmly rooted in God's instructions to His people about how to remain loyal to Him and how to teach their children to do the same. Read the passage below to better understand Saul's faith upbringing and how it shaped his life.

Deuteronomy 6:4–12, 20–25 NRSV

Hear, O Israel: The Lord is our God, the Lord alone. You shall love the Lord your God with all your heart, and with all your soul, and with all your might. Keep these words that I am commanding you today in your heart. Recite them to your children and talk about them when you are at home and when you are away, when you lie down and when you rise. Bind them as a sign on your hand, fix them as an emblem on your forehead, and write them on the doorposts of your house and on your gates.

When the Lord your God has brought you into the land that He swore to your ancestors, to Abraham, to Isaac, and to Jacob, to give you—a land with fine, large cities that you did not build, houses filled with all sorts of goods that you did not fill, hewn cisterns that you did not hew, vineyards and olive groves that you did not plant—and when you have eaten your fill, take care that you do not forget the Lord, who brought you out of the land of Egypt, out of the house of slavery. . . .

When your children ask you in time to come, "What is the meaning of the decrees and the statutes and the ordinances that the Lord our God has commanded you?" then you shall say to your children, "We were Pharaoh's slaves in Egypt, but the Lord brought us out of Egypt with a mighty hand. The Lord displayed before our eyes great and awesome signs and wonders against Egypt, against Pharaoh and all his household. He brought us out from there in order to bring us in, to give us the land that He promised on oath to our ancestors. Then the Lord commanded us to observe all these statutes, to fear the Lord our God, for our lasting good, so as to keep us alive, as is now the case. If we diligently observe this entire commandment before the Lord our God, as He has commanded us, we will be in the right."

LET'S REVIEW

Saul was a Pharisee, the son of a Pharisee. Based on today's reading, what are some adjectives you might use to describe the Pharisees?

Tarsus was on a major trade route between Cilicia and Syria, which led merchants from diverse backgrounds to the city. How do you think Saul's upbringing around people whose cultures and ways of thinking were different from his helped prepare him to serve as a missionary?

In Deuteronomy 6, God warns His people not to forget Him. Why is it tempting to wander away from God when things are going well for us?

APPLICATION

From the moment of his birth, Saul was caught between the two worlds into which he was born—the Roman world of his hometown, Tarsus, and the world of Pharisaical Judaism. There must have been countless times during his upbringing when he struggled to balance the two. Yet it was this crucible of warring cultural influences that uniquely equipped him to take the Gospel to the Gentiles.

We have little control over the world in which we live. Even the most carefully planned life may take a sharp turn onto a painful road that we would have never chosen, leaving us no choice but to navigate it as best as we can. There is tremendous hope in trusting that God is willing and able to use our circumstances, whatever they are, to equip us to fulfill His unique purpose in our lives, if only we will surrender them to Him.

Our God is a God of redemption. He doesn't waste anything.

one true God

PROMPT

Write a prayer to God asking Him to help you see your current circumstances as the thing shaping you for your future purpose.

DIG DEEPER

Deuteronomy 12:28
Matthew 22:34–37
Isaiah 9:6–7

DAY 2

Son of a Pharisee

The synagogue is quiet and still. The benches lining the walls are empty.

"Moses' Seat," a low chair carved from stone, rests in the center of the room. It is from this place of honor that the rabbis read from the Law and the Prophets.

The temple in Jerusalem is the center of Judaism, the place where heaven and earth meet, the holy site from which God reveals Himself to His people. For the Jews scattered throughout the Roman Empire and living far from the Holy City after the return from Babylonian exile, the synagogue is the center of the community's spiritual life. It serves as a tether to the temple, the Torah, and most importantly, to the one true God.

At this time of day, the synagogue is vacant as the members of the Jewish community attend to their jobs and homes, but in a smaller building next door, important work is underway. This is the bet midrash, the house of learning, where Jewish boys study the Torah.

This day, a gathering of young boys sits at the feet of a rabbi, hearing the story of God's special relationship with their ancestors.

We are the children of Abraham.

God chose us to be His people, set apart from all others, to worship Him alone.

God rescued us from Egyptian slavery and gave us a land of our own, but our ancestors weren't loyal to Him. They rejected the God who saved them to bow at the feet of idols, so God allowed our ancestors to be taken away into Babylonian exile.

After seventy years, God rescued His people and returned them to their homes, but now, slavery has descended on us once again. The Romans rule over us, occupying our land. Once again, we await God's deliverance.

Therefore, we honor the temple and study the Torah. We must remain faithful to our God, for the time is drawing near when He has promised to rescue us again.

The children all listen attentively, but one little boy, Saul, stands out among the rest. He absorbs the Law, the Prophets, and the Psalms with lightning speed. His curious mind never rests, whether he is memorizing God's Word or learning to read and write Hebrew, Aramaic, and Greek.

Saul is always listening, always asking questions, always making connections.

His mind is insatiable both in the *bet midrash* and as he sits beside his father's workbench. Saul observes his father, a Pharisee, ceremonially wash his hands before eating. Saul takes note as he carefully measures out a tenth of his spices so that he might tithe even the smallest resource. He watches him secure a phylactery, a small box filled with bits of scroll inscribed with God's law, to his forehead and another to his arm with long strips of leather.

Saul listens as his father prays without ceasing, weaving his loyalty to God into the fabric of his life. Bit by bit, he begins to understand his role in Israel's story: If he and his people want to break free of Roman occupation, they must remain perfectly faithful to God, temple, and Torah.

As Saul leaves his boyhood behind, this belief will grow in his heart and mind until he comes to the conviction that any hint of disloyalty from his fellow Jews must be corrected by any means necessary, including flogging, imprisonment . . .

And even death.

SCRIPTURE READING

The Pharisees had a noble goal: keep Israel faithful to God. When they lost sight of God's heart behind the law, however, they began to hurt others in their pursuit of perfection. Read what Jesus had to say about this in the passage below.

Mark 7:1–13 NRSV

Now when the Pharisees and some of the scribes who had come from Jerusalem gathered around Him, they noticed that some of His disciples were eating with defiled hands, that is, without washing them. (For the Pharisees, and all the Jews, do not eat unless they thoroughly wash their hands, thus observing the tradition of the elders; and they do not eat anything from the market unless they wash it; and there are also many other traditions that they observe, the washing of cups, pots, and bronze kettles.) So the Pharisees and the scribes asked Him, "Why do Your disciples not live according to the tradition of the elders, but eat with defiled hands?" He said to them, "Isaiah prophesied rightly about you hypocrites, as it is written,

> 'This people honors Me with their lips,
> but their hearts are far from Me;
> in vain do they worship Me,
> teaching human precepts as doctrines.'
> You abandon the commandment of God and hold to human tradition."

Then He said to them, "You have a fine way of rejecting the commandment of God in order to keep your tradition! For Moses said, 'Honor your father and your mother'; and, 'Whoever speaks evil of father or mother must surely die.' But you say that if anyone tells father or mother, 'Whatever support you might have had from me is Corban' (that is, an offering to God)—then you no longer permit doing anything for a father or mother, thus making void the word of God through your tradition that you have handed on. And you do many things like this."

LET'S REVIEW

The Pharisees began with the best intentions—to keep Israel faithful to God's law. For what did they abandon God's commandments, according to Jesus?

The Pharisees were considered the spiritual leaders who most accurately interpreted the law. This is what motivated them to build "hedges" around each law. The idea was to establish so many standards around the law that one would have to break them all before he was in danger of violating the law itself. (This is what Jesus called "traditions" in today's reading.) The problem with the Pharisees' "hedges" arose when they began to judge each other on how well they kept these man-made rules.

How have you seen a spirit of judgment cause harm in the church?

One of Jesus' criticisms of the Pharisees was that "they tie up heavy burdens, hard to bear, and lay them on the shoulders of others; but they themselves are unwilling to lift a finger to move them" (Matthew 23:4 NRSV).

What do you think Jesus meant by this statement?

APPLICATION

As the son of a Pharisee, Saul was taught the importance of faithfulness to God's law from an early age. Sadly, as Saul and other Pharisees narrowed their focus to perfectly keeping God's law, they lost the heart behind it. Instead of the law showing them how to love God and love their neighbors, it became a weapon they used to mercilessly judge each other.

Although Saul could not see the danger in this as a young Pharisee, we know that the "law of love" came to mean everything to him. In his great letter to the Corinthians, we find this powerful proclamation: "And now faith, hope, and love abide, these three; and the greatest of these is love" (I Corinthians 13:13 NRSV).

Saul will make the dramatic transformation from judgment to love, but he will inflict incredible harm on the followers of the Messiah before that happens.

Our God is a God of love. Nothing matters more to Him than how we imitate that love in our relationships with each other. May we seek Him humbly in prayer, asking Him to give us a heart like His.

heaven and earth meet

PROMPT

We all fall into the temptation to pass judgment on each other. Take a moment to think about how this plays out in your own life right now. Then write a prayer about that situation, asking God to give you a heart of love instead of a heart of judgment.

DIG DEEPER

Matthew 12:1–8
Matthew 23:23–24
Matthew 22:36–40

DAY 3

Zeal

Sitting at the feet of his rabbi, Saul's senses are filled with the rhythms of Jerusalem. Beneath him, he feels the smooth, perfectly hewn stones of the temple courtyard. As he lifts his eyes to survey the temple courts, he sees the towering walls encircle the space, inset with porticos from which Roman soldiers keep a watchful eye on their Jewish subjects.

Saul hears merchants haggling with worshipers as they purchase animals for sacrifice, the cooing of doves and bleating of lambs, the clink of coins as they drop into the collection boxes, and the ceaseless drone of countless prayers.

Above it all is the voice of his rabbi, the esteemed Gamaliel. Under his tutelage, Saul is receiving the best education available to a young Jewish man, but something inside him turns away from his teacher. When Gamaliel encourages tolerance, Saul bristles.

How could he speak of tolerance when Israel languishes under the boot of Rome? When the time for God's deliverance is drawing near? While so many of his fellow Jews are falling short in keeping God's law?

Saul is a young man now, poised to take on the world. His brilliant mind has been honed to razor sharpness by years of studying the Torah. A lifetime of hearing the stories of his ancestors has set his heart on fire with fierce loyalty to the one true God.

He is sure of his convictions and confident in his purpose. He is ready to unleash a purifying fire on his own people if that is what it takes for them to remain faithful.

Saul looks into the gentle eyes of Gamaliel, then into the mocking faces of the Roman soldiers looking down on him from the porticoes, their hands clasping the hilts of their swords. The time for tolerance has passed.

What Israel needs is zeal.

Zeal like that of Phineas, who wielded his sword to cleanse the Israelite camp of idolatry as they journeyed to the land God promised to Abraham. Zeal like that of Elijah on Mount Carmel, where fire rained from heaven and the prophets of Baal were scattered and slain.

The fire of zeal burns hotter and hotter in Saul's heart until it consumes all else. It incinerates love and mercy for his neighbors until all memory of their humanity lies in ashes. The fire of zeal rages and roars until Saul finds himself capable of justifying anything and everything in its name.

SCRIPTURE READING

Saul, and many other Pharisees, were strict in their observance of the law, but Jesus challenged His disciples to move beyond the letter of the law to the heart. As you read the Scripture below, think about how Paul would have felt if he was one of the Pharisees listening to Jesus.

Matthew 5:17–22 NRSV

Do not think that I have come to abolish the law or the prophets; I have come not to abolish but to fulfill. For truly I tell you, until heaven and earth pass away, not one letter, not one stroke of a letter, will pass from the law until all is accomplished. Therefore, whoever breaks one of the least of these commandments, and teaches others to do the same, will be called least in the kingdom of heaven; but whoever does them and teaches them will be called great in the kingdom of heaven. For I tell you, unless your righteousness exceeds that of the scribes and Pharisees, you will never enter the kingdom of heaven.

You have heard that it was said to those of ancient times, "You shall not murder"; and "whoever murders shall be liable to judgment." But I say to you that if you are angry with a brother or sister, you will be liable to judgment; and if you insult a brother or sister, you will be liable to the council; and if you say, "You fool," you will be liable to the hell of fire.

Imagine you were sitting next to Jesus' disciples when He told them their righteousness must exceed that of the Pharisees, who were incredibly strict in their obedience to the law. How would you feel?

Jesus warned His disciples about harboring anger toward their brothers and sisters. How would this admonition challenge Saul's attitude toward those he felt weren't following the law closely enough?

In verses 21-22, Jesus warns His followers about the danger of contempt. Most of us struggle with feelings of contempt for others from time to time. What are some ways you can guard against contempt for others in your life?

APPLICATION

It isn't a very long journey from a sincere desire for righteousness to a place of judgment.

In his book *Yeshua: A Guide to the Real Jesus and the Original Church*, Dr. Ron Moseley warns us that before we look down on the Pharisees for how they slipped into judgment, we need to consider a few of the ways the modern church has done the same:

> Before condemning the Pharisees for their many rigid and excessive traditions, Christians should first look back over church history, and not so very long ago. It was only one hundred years ago that D.L. Moody preached against the sin of men wearing ruffled shirts. During that same period Maria Woodworth-Etter was famous for teaching that women who did not wear long sleeves were sinners. Around the turn of the twentieth century, Billy Sunday preached that it was a sin for women to chew gum, and some considered it a sin to whistle.

Each generation, it seems, finds an issue for which we feel entitled to condemn others.

Jesus was forever pointing His followers back to the *heart* of the law: Love God and love your neighbor.

If we are honest, the impulse to judge each other is pretty tempting for most of us. It feels so much better to take inventory of our brothers and sisters' perceived shortcomings than to honestly—and courageously—face the secret motivations and attitudes in our own hearts.

The key to quieting a judgmental spirit is to humbly trust God with our neighbors' obedience. The Almighty has it under control. He doesn't need our help keeping order.

Once we do this, we are free to pursue the greatest challenge of all—loving our neighbors as ourselves.

Zeal

Jesus says we violate the command not to murder when we are "angry with [our] brother without a cause" (Matthew 5:22 NKJV). Are you holding on to bitterness against someone? Write a prayer below asking God to give you a heart of love and forgiveness for that person.

DIG DEEPER

Matthew 7:1–5
John 13:34–35
James 5:9

DAY 4

The Stoning of Stephen

An angry crowd, armed with dishonest witnesses and trumped-up charges, gathered before the Sanhedrin, the Jewish religious court, to present their case against Stephen, one of the followers of Jesus.

For days, Stephen's accusers had tried valiantly to disprove his claim that Jesus was the Messiah but had been unable to do so. Over and again, they found themselves frustrated and thrown off balance by Stephen's logic, his deft use of rhetoric, and his command of the Scriptures. It was almost as if some otherworldly power was empowering his defense. It was clear that if they were going to silence Stephen, it would take something more drastic.

An accusation of blasphemy against both God and Moses would surely get the job done.

After the false witnesses had spun their stories for the court, it was Stephen's turn to present his defense. If his accusers were intent on charging him with blasphemy against Moses and God, he would show them that his foundation in their shared faith was solid. Step by step, he retold the audience the story of their ancestors, of how God chose Israel to be His people,

delivered them from Egyptian slavery, and gave them the law through Moses.

Then, with the foundation of his defense laid, Stephen went on the offensive.

He leveled a steely gaze at the Jewish religious court and delivered his own charges against *them*, using the same words God had so often used with their ancestors.

Stephen called them "stiff-necked." He told them their hearts and ears were "uncircumcised."

He said that just like their ancestors had persecuted and killed the prophets, so they had murdered the Messiah.

A roar of rage filled the room as Stephen's accusers seized him and dragged him from the court and into the street.

The mob, wild-eyed and crazed with fury, stampeded through Jerusalem, their angry shouts echoing off the stone walls of the palatial mansions of the wealthy and the humbler homes of peasants. When Stephen, at the center of the fray, stumbled and fell, rough hands clawed at his robes, forced him back to his feet, and then pushed him forward, on and on until, at last, they were outside of the city.

Soon, the mob arrived at Beth haSeqilah, the place of the stoning.

Saul was there too. He stood back from the cliff edge, far enough away not to see the rocky terrain below but close enough to oversee the execution. One by one, men stepped away from the rabble to lay their cloaks at Saul's feet for safekeeping as they prepared for the task at hand.

The first witness pushed Stephen over the edge of the cliff. The second threw the first stone down upon him. Then, the mob joined in, and stones fell like rain.

Stephen looked up to heaven and prayed.

He didn't ask for mercy or a thousand angelic hosts to come to his rescue. He didn't ask God for justice or for vengeance on his assailants.

Instead, following the example of Jesus as He hung on the cross, Stephen entrusted his spirit to the God who raises the dead and asked for mercy for the men who were taking his life one stone at a time.

In a matter of minutes, it was all over. Stephen's body lay lifeless. The crowd quieted, retrieved their cloaks from the ground at Saul's feet, and dispersed, self-satisfied and sure of the "justice" they had rendered.

Saul turned away from Beth haSeqilah toward Jerusalem with a new focus for the zeal that burned within him. The followers of Jesus had to be stopped. He would cleanse Israel of this new blasphemy no matter how far he had to go.

And he would begin in Damascus.

SCRIPTURE READING

Read what the Bible says about the stoning of Stephen.

Acts 6:8–15; 7:51–60 NRSV

Stephen Is Taken Before the Sanhedrin

Stephen, full of grace and power, did great wonders and signs among the people. Then some of those who belonged to the synagogue of the Freedmen (as it was called), Cyrenians, Alexandrians, and others of those from Cilicia and Asia, stood up and argued with Stephen. But they could not withstand the wisdom and the Spirit with which he spoke. Then they secretly instigated some men to say, "We have heard him speak blasphemous words against Moses and God." They stirred up the people as well as the elders and the scribes; then they suddenly confronted him, seized him, and brought him before the council. They set up false witnesses who said, "This man never stops saying things against this holy place and the law; for we have heard him say that this Jesus of Nazareth will destroy this place and will change the customs that Moses handed on to us." And all who sat in the council looked intently at him, and they saw that his face was like the face of an angel.

Stephen's Speech to the Council

". . . You stiff-necked people, uncircumcised in heart and ears, you are forever opposing the Holy Spirit, just as your ancestors used to do. Which of the prophets did your ancestors not persecute? They killed those who foretold the coming of the Righteous One, and now you have become His betrayers and murderers. You are the ones that received the law as ordained by angels, and yet you have not kept it."

The Stoning of Stephen

When they heard these things, they became enraged and ground their teeth at Stephen. But filled with the Holy Spirit, he gazed into heaven and saw the glory of God and Jesus standing at the right hand of God. "Look," he said, "I see the heavens opened and the Son of Man standing at the right hand of God!" But they covered their ears, and with a loud shout all rushed together against him. Then they dragged him out of the city and began to stone him; and the witnesses laid their coats at the feet of a young man named Saul. While they were stoning Stephen, he prayed, "Lord Jesus, receive my spirit." Then he knelt down and cried out in a loud voice, "Lord, do not hold this sin against them." When he had said this, he died.

LET'S REVIEW

Stephen called the religious leaders "stiff-necked." This was a colorful term God used at times to describe the Israelites. It was His way of saying they were stubborn!

How does stubbornness get in the way of God doing His good work in our hearts?

Circumcision was the primary symbol of God's covenant, or relationship, with Abraham and his descendants. Stephen accused the religious leaders of being "uncircumcised in heart and ears." They strove to follow God's rules but neglected their relationship with Him.

What do you think are some of the dangers of separating the precepts in God's Word from a close, vibrant relationship with our loving Father?

The stoning of Stephen was in violation of both Jewish and Roman law. When Stephen's executioners took his life under the pretense of defending the law, they were, in fact, breaking the law themselves.

In Matthew 7, Jesus warns that we must first eradicate our own sin before we turn our attention to our neighbor's faults. Considering this, do you think there is ever room for us to weigh in on what our neighbor should or shouldn't do? Why or why not?

APPLICATION

Circumcision was the primary symbol of the covenantal relationship between the Jews and God. When we approach God with *uncircumcised hearts and ears*, we are no longer practicing faith, but religion. Faith is relational—it starts with a relationship with God that is then worked out in our relationships with each other.

When we reduce this relationship to our own understanding—what we have reasoned out to be right and wrong, righteous and unrighteous, without first and foremost humbly seeking God to hear His voice and obey it—we will inevitably leave the open spaces of covenantal relationship and set up camp in the barren wilderness of religion, where there is no room for love, mercy, or grace.

Communion with God through covenantal relationship will always challenge us to think more honestly and deeply about our own sin instead of our neighbor's. The more we seek God's face, the more we realize the immensity of His grace extended to us through Jesus Christ. Our gratitude for this lavish gift softens our hearts and opens our ears.

Grace always draws us near to Jesus.

be brave now. Be strong

PROMPT

Where has your heart become hardened to God's leading and your ears deaf to His voice? In what ways can you be more open to following His plan for you?

DIG DEEPER

Deuteronomy 10:12–16
Psalm 73:6–8
Matthew 13:10–17

DAY 5

The Road to Damascus

Clip-clop, clip-clop.

All was silent except for the steady percussion of donkey hooves striking the road. In the beginning, the long, monotonous hours between Jerusalem and Damascus had been filled with lively conversation between Saul and his traveling companions. The many days on the road, however, had lulled the men into a sort of trance, each of them lost in their own thoughts.

For Saul, it was a time to ponder the mission before him and the work he had left behind in Jerusalem. With the backing of Caiaphas, the high priest, Saul had already rounded up many followers of "The Way," the men and women who believed the ridiculous notion that Jesus had been the Messiah long promised by God.

A crucified Messiah? It was absurd! When the Messiah came, He would do so with power and might. A victorious warrior, the Messiah would cleanse the land of Roman occupation and return Israel to her former glory.

Now, with letters of authority from Caiaphas in his hands, and the midday sun beating down on his head, Saul was on his way to the great city of Damascus. He would purge the large Jewish community there of this blasphemous influence before it had the chance to take root.

Time was of the essence. Damascus, home to several synagogues, not only bustled with commerce that drew people from far away, but it also sat at the crossroads of three major trade routes. If the followers of Jesus began to spread their message there, visitors to the city would hear it and then take it back to their homes. Like a bit of yeast in a bowl of bread dough, the movement would grow and spread until it was no longer containable.

Clip-clop, clip-clop.

With the rhythm of the donkey beneath him, Saul pondered, and Saul prayed. *Hear, O Israel. The Lord our God, the Lord is one.*

Saul couldn't remember a time when praying the Shema wasn't woven into his life, shaping him into the devout, zeal-filled man he had become. Now he prayed it with each breath as the long miles passed beneath him, and the donkey swayed.

The Shema had taught him what was nonnegotiable—loyalty to the one true God. Consequently, His temple in Jerusalem, the place where heaven and earth met and God revealed Himself to His people, was sacred. Nothing mattered more than faithfulness to God, the Torah, and the temple. Now these followers of "The Way" were proclaiming that the temple was only a temporary symbol pointing to Jesus of Nazareth, the true place heaven and earth met. To Saul, this was blasphemy of the highest order, and he was determined to snuff out the embers of the movement before it burst into an uncontrollable flame.

Suddenly, a dazzling light flashed all around Saul and his companions. They fell to the ground, trembling and dazed, as a voice rang out from heaven.

"Saul, Saul, why are you persecuting Me? It hurts you to kick against the goads." It was Jesus, a Messiah who had indeed been crucified, but who had risen from the grave with the keys of sin, hell, and death in His hands. His was a greater victory than Saul could have ever imagined.

When the voice ceased and the light faded, Saul was cast into absolute darkness. He was blind.

As he struggled to his feet, he began to grapple with the realization that being loyal to the one true God didn't mean faithfulness to the temple, but to Jesus. He had a new mission as well. Jesus wanted him to join forces with the very people he had been persecuting in spreading the good news that the Messiah had come.

Jesus wanted Saul to preach that message not only to his fellow Jews, but to the Gentiles as well.

Saul's friends helped him back onto his donkey and led him to Damascus, sightless, but with a clear vision of just how wrong he had been.

SCRIPTURE READING

Saul's conversion story appears three times in Scripture, but the most complete account occurs when he testifies before King Agrippa after his arrest at the temple in Jerusalem (Acts 21). Read the passage below to better grasp the significance of this life-changing moment in Saul's life.

Acts 26:9–18 NRSV

Indeed, I myself was convinced that I ought to do many things against the name of Jesus of Nazareth. And that is what I did in Jerusalem; with authority received from the chief priests, I not only locked up many of the saints in prison, but I also cast my vote against them when they were being condemned to death. By punishing them often in all the synagogues I tried to force them to blaspheme; and since I was so furiously enraged at them, I pursued them even to foreign cities.

With this in mind, I was travelling to Damascus with the authority and commission of the chief priests, when at midday along the road, your Excellency, I saw a light from heaven, brighter than the sun, shining around me and my companions. When we had all fallen to the ground, I heard a voice saying to me in the Hebrew language, "Saul, Saul, why are you persecuting me? It hurts you to kick against the goads." I asked, "Who are you, Lord?" The Lord answered, "I am Jesus whom you are persecuting. But get up and stand on your feet; for I have appeared to you for this purpose, to appoint you to serve and testify to the things in which you have seen Me and to those in which I will appear to you. I will rescue you from your people and from the Gentiles—to whom I am sending you to open their eyes so that they may turn from darkness to light and from the power of Satan to God, so that they may receive forgiveness of sins and a place among those who are sanctified by faith in Me."

LET'S REVIEW

It is impossible to overstate the significance of the temple during Saul's lifetime. It was not only where, Jews believed, heaven and earth met and God revealed Himself to His people, but it was also the headquarters of the Jewish court and the center of commerce in Jerusalem. For Saul and his contemporaries, loyalty to the temple was intertwined with loyalty to God. What dangers lie in putting our trust in institutions and those who lead them above our trust in God?

Jesus stated that it hurt Saul to "kick against the goads." A goad was a sharp, pointed stick used for driving livestock; the more the animal resisted his master's leading, the more painful the process became. Think about a time when you resisted God's leading in your life. If you could write to your younger self, what advice would you give?

In this statement about "kicking against the goads," Jesus referenced a Greek parable about the danger of resisting the divine will. This is precisely what Saul's rabbi, Gamaliel, warned his fellow members of the Jewish council about concerning the followers of Jesus: "I tell you, keep away from these men and let them alone; because if this plan or this undertaking is of human origin, it will fail; but if it is of God, you will not be able to overthrow them—in that case you may even be found fighting against God!" (Acts 5:38–39 NRSV) What do you think Gamaliel believed about God that allowed him to resist the temptation to control his neighbor?

APPLICATION

In Isaiah 55:8–9, God warned His wayward people against the danger of assuming that His purposes, and even His way of thinking, were anything at all like theirs:

> For My thoughts are not your thoughts,
> nor are your ways My ways, says the LORD.
> For as the heavens are higher than the earth,
> so are My ways higher than your ways
> and My thoughts than your thoughts. (NRSV)

Gamaliel and Saul were both men who took their faith seriously. Gamaliel's faith in the mighty power of God freed him from the need to control others. Saul's faith drove him to hold others to his standard of holiness, with devastating consequences.

Proverbs 1:7 says that the fear of God is the beginning of wisdom. The word *fear* means a holy respect, an understanding that God's thoughts and ways are not like ours at all. Gamaliel was right. God is wise enough to know what is best and powerful enough to see it through. We can trust Him with others when they are making choices that seem unwise and even destructive.

God has it all under control, and the truth is, no matter how hard we try, we never do. In attempting to control others, we run the risk of causing terrible harm and exhausting ourselves in the process.

Don't resist the divine will. Kicking against the goads is painful. You are a child of the eternal, almighty God. Rest in Him.

Have you ever had a sharp transition? When you were thinking one way and then something caused you to change your mind? Write about your experience, and think about how Paul felt when he was surrounded by light and heard the voice of Jesus.

DIG DEEPER

John 2:18–22
Acts 8:1–4
I Corinthians 5:9–10

DAY 6

Three Days in the Dark

Darkness.

Three days pass without sight, but the inky midnight before Saul's eyes can't begin to compare to the shadow that has fallen over his mind and heart.

Saul's friends bring him food and water, but he refuses it. Instead, he ponders. He prays.

He grieves over what he has done.

The frightened faces of the men and women he persecuted float through his memories. He thinks of Stephen praying that God would have mercy on his assailants, including Saul, even as the stones fell.

Stephen had gazed up into the throne room of God and saw Jesus sitting at the right hand of God, while Saul, who thought he knew and understood so much, saw nothing. Now Saul's spiritual blindness has been replaced with a physical one, but, with brutal clarity, his heart now perceives the truth.

The Messiah was nothing like Saul supposed He would be. He hadn't ridden into Jerusalem on a war horse to wipe the Romans from the face of the earth, but on a gentle donkey to save them. This Messiah wasn't concerned with politics and power. He came to redeem all creation from the curse.

Saul realizes much too late that his vision of redemption was too stingy, too small.

He thinks back through the Law, the Prophets, and the Psalms, weaving the new, earth-shattering reality of Jesus the Messiah into it all. Suddenly, He is everywhere. How could Saul have missed it?

How could he have been so . . . *blind?*

On the third day, there is a knock at the door. A man named Ananias has come, saying that God has sent him. He approaches Saul, lays his hands on him, and prays that he might receive his sight and be filled with the Holy Spirit.

Immediately, Saul's eyes are opened, and his heart is made new.

Saul looks into Ananias' eyes and finds compassion mixed with fear. Word of Saul's ruthless persecution of the followers of Christ had preceded him to Damascus. If Jesus had not intercepted Saul along the way, Ananias' meeting with him would have unfolded very differently. Ananias has good reason to fear the man before him.

And yet he calls Saul "brother."

Grace, unfathomable grace. Mercy replaces vengeance. Division is wiped away by brotherhood.

The Messiah has come.

SCRIPTURE READING

During the three days Saul sat in darkness waiting for Ananias, he had the chance to rethink what it meant to be faithful to God now that the Messiah had come and to process the harm he had caused in his spiritual blindness. Read the scriptural account of those three days.

Acts 9:8–21 NRSV

Saul got up from the ground, and though his eyes were open, he could see nothing; so they led him by the hand and brought him into Damascus. For three days he was without sight, and neither ate nor drank.

Now there was a disciple in Damascus named Ananias. The Lord said to him in a vision, "Ananias." He answered, "Here I am, Lord." The Lord said to him, "Get up and go to the street called Straight, and at the house of Judas look for a man of Tarsus named Saul. At this moment he is praying, and he has seen in a vision a man named Ananias come in and lay his hands on him so that he might regain his sight." But Ananias answered, "Lord, I have heard from many about this man, how much evil he has done to your saints in Jerusalem; and here he has authority from the chief priests to bind all who invoke Your name." But the Lord said to him, "Go, for he is an instrument whom I have chosen to bring My name before Gentiles and kings and before the people of Israel; I myself will show him how much he must suffer for the sake of My name." So Ananias went and entered the house. He laid his hands on Saul and said, "Brother Saul, the Lord Jesus, who appeared to you on your way here, has sent me so that you may regain your sight and be filled with the Holy Spirit." And immediately something like scales fell from his eyes, and his sight was restored. Then he got up and was baptized, and after taking some food, he regained his strength.

For several days he was with the disciples in Damascus, and immediately he began to proclaim Jesus in the synagogues, saying, "He is the Son of God." All who heard him were amazed and said, "Is not this the man who made havoc in Jerusalem among those who invoked this name? And has he not come here for the purpose of bringing them bound before the chief priests?"

What was Ananias' first reaction when God sent him to Saul? How would you feel if you were asked by God to face someone with such a reputation?

Jesus was very different from the Messiah Saul had envisioned, especially because He was crucified. For Jews living at the time of Saul, it was unthinkable that the Messiah would complete His work of salvation through sacrifice rather than conquest.

How do you think this new understanding of the Messiah helped prepare Saul to "suffer" in the name of the Lord as he proclaimed the Gospel (Acts 9:16)?

Saul had always been so confident, but as he waited in darkness for those three days, he was suddenly incredibly vulnerable, both physically and spiritually. How do you think that vulnerability helped prepare his heart for Ananias' arrival?

APPLICATION

What happens when Jesus shows up in our lives and looks nothing like what we expect?

This is what happened to Saul on the road to Damascus. Saul loved the idea of a militant Messiah, one who would purge the Romans from Israel with brutal efficiency. Instead, the Messiah came to give His life in the most painful, humiliating way possible so that the Romans could be part of God's family too.

Much later in his ministry, Saul would sum up the problem of a crucified Messiah in his first letter to the Corinthians:

"Jews demand signs and Greeks look for wisdom, but we preach Christ crucified: a stumbling block to Jews and foolishness to Gentiles, but to those whom God has called, both Jews and Greeks, Christ the power of God and the wisdom of God" (I Corinthians 1:22–24 NIV).

It is human nature to prefer might instead of sacrifice, and most of us fall into the temptation to force our beliefs (not necessarily God's truth, but *our* beliefs) on others at some point in our lives. When we do, let's face those tendencies honestly, and ask God to give us sacrificial, loving, radically forgiving hearts just like His.

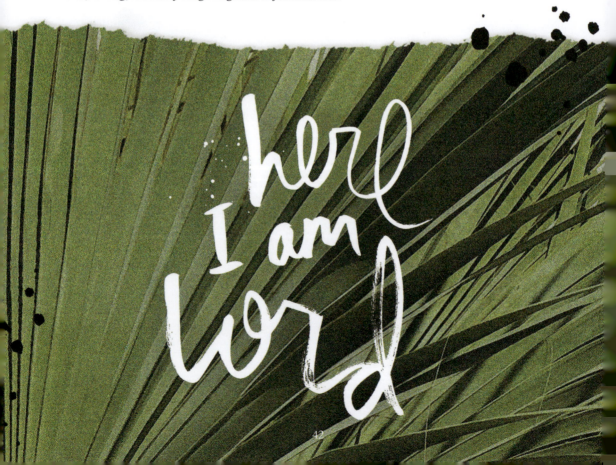

here I am Lord

PROMPT

Courageously ask God to show you relationships in your life in which you are facing the impulse to control rather than follow Christ's example of redeeming love. Write a prayer to God and ask Him to change your heart.

DIG DEEPER

I Corinthians 15:9–10
Ephesians 3:1–12
I Timothy 1:12–17

DAY 7

Pilgrimage

By day, the heat was relentless. With the cloudless dome of the sky above, and a sea of sand below, Saul's donkey trudged steadily onward weaving its way through bare, jagged mountains.

When the sun dropped beneath the horizon each evening, the temperature plummeted. Saul huddled close to the donkey's side for warmth and stared up into the sweeping night sky, strewn with thousands upon thousands of stars.

Day, after night, after day, the cycle repeated as Sinai, the mountain of God, steadily grew closer.

Sinai. The mountain where, as Moses led the children of Israel out of Egypt, God affirmed His covenant with them and gave them the law.

Sinai. Where Elijah, another zealous man of God, had once fled, discouraged, disillusioned, and alone when his life, too, had turned upside down. There in a cave on the mountainside, God met with his weary prophet, Elijah, in the holy silence of Sinai to encourage and renew him, and to recommission him for his purpose and the work that remained.

Now Saul followed in Elijah's footsteps to seek God's face, recommit himself to God, and discover what it meant to be faithful now that he knew Jesus was the Messiah.

Finally, sunburned and weary, Saul stood at the base of the mountain. Somewhere, far above him, God had spoken to Moses face-to-face, giving him the law. And there, on the plain surrounding the base of the mountain, the twelve tribes of Israel had once set up camp and committed themselves to obey God, then immediately betrayed Him by fashioning a golden calf to worship instead. And somewhere, in one of the caves dotting the mountainside, was where God met with Elijah and commissioned him to announce Israel's new king.

On Sinai, the place of covenant and new beginnings, Saul met with God. Afterward, when he turned his donkey back toward Damascus, he, like Elijah, did so with a new mission: Saul would proclaim the advent of Israel's new king. But this time her King was the Lord of all creation.

King Jesus, the Messiah, would reign forever. He would be called Wonderful, Counselor, Mighty God, Everlasting Father, Prince of Peace, and His kingdom would have no end.

SCRIPTURE READING

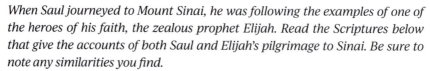

When Saul journeyed to Mount Sinai, he was following the examples of one of the heroes of his faith, the zealous prophet Elijah. Read the Scriptures below that give the accounts of both Saul and Elijah's pilgrimage to Sinai. Be sure to note any similarities you find.

Elijah Meets God at Sinai (I Kings 19:9–18 NRSV)

At that place he came to a cave, and spent the night there.

Then the word of the Lord came to him, saying, "What are you doing here, Elijah?" He answered, "I have been very zealous for the Lord, the God of hosts; for the Israelites have forsaken your covenant, thrown down your altars, and killed your prophets with the sword. I alone am left, and they are seeking my life, to take it away."

He said, "Go out and stand on the mountain before the Lord, for the Lord is about to pass by." Now there was a great wind, so strong that it was splitting mountains and breaking rocks in pieces before the Lord, but the Lord was not in the wind; and after the wind an earthquake, but the Lord was not in the earthquake; and after the earthquake a fire, but the Lord was not in the fire; and after the fire a sound of sheer silence. When Elijah heard it, he wrapped his face in his mantle and went out and stood at the entrance of the cave. Then there came a voice to him that said, "What are you doing here, Elijah?" He answered, "I have been very zealous for the Lord, the God of hosts; for the Israelites have forsaken your covenant, thrown down your altars, and killed your prophets with the sword. I alone am left, and they are seeking my life, to take it away." Then the Lord said to him, "Go, return on your way to the wilderness of Damascus; when you arrive, you shall anoint Hazael as king over Aram. Also you shall anoint Jehu son of Nimshi as king over Israel; and you shall anoint Elisha son of Shaphat of Abel-meholah as prophet in your place. Whoever escapes from the sword of Hazael, Jehu shall kill; and whoever escapes from the sword of Jehu, Elisha shall kill. Yet I will leave seven thousand in Israel, all the knees that have not bowed to Baal, and every mouth that has not kissed him."

Saul Recounts His Pilgrimage to Sinai (Galatians 1:14–17 NRSV)

I advanced in Judaism beyond many among my people of the same age, for I was far more zealous for the traditions of my ancestors. But when God, who had set me apart before I was born and called me through His grace, was pleased to reveal His Son to me, so that I might proclaim Him among the Gentiles, I did not confer with any human being, nor did I go up to Jerusalem to those who were already apostles before me, but I went away at once into Arabia, and afterwards I returned to Damascus.

LET'S REVIEW

Elijah arrived at the mountain of God mentally and physically exhausted. God sent an angel to minister to Elijah's physical needs before He addressed his emotional and spiritual needs (I Kings 19:5–8).

How does knowing that God tenderly cared for Elijah's physical needs before addressing his discouragement and doubt affect you?

One of the most heart-wrenching statements in today's reading is when Elijah said to God, "I alone am left." Both Saul and Elijah came to Sinai in need of refreshment and encouragement.

When did you last feel discouraged? Were you able to take the time you needed to rest and meet with God? If so, write about that experience below. If not, imagine how things could have turned out differently if you had.

We live in a world of noise and constant entertainment. How do you think this keeps us from hearing the voice of God?

APPLICATION

We all have had times when it felt like our lives were spinning out of control, when we lost focus and a bit of our true selves along the way. When we get face-to-face with God, He shows us the big picture, what we can't see when we are wounded, beaten down, and weary.

Sometimes we must stop the merry-go-round of life and intentionally seek out a place where we can commune with God without interruption so that He can get us back on track. This isn't indulgence. This is taking our relationship with God—and how that relationship works itself out in our realm of influence—seriously.

Often, when we look back on these times, we find they are important faith landmarks, after which neither we nor our faith are ever the same.

First Kings 19:13 tells us that Elijah covered his face with his mantle before approaching God. Perhaps some of us hesitate to get face-to-face with God because it can be terrifying to encounter such infinite power and glory.

Our mighty God, however, is also a God of love. He wants to meet with us. He wants to know us, and for us to know Him in return.

God reveals Himself to us in the quiet spaces we consecrate for Him alone.

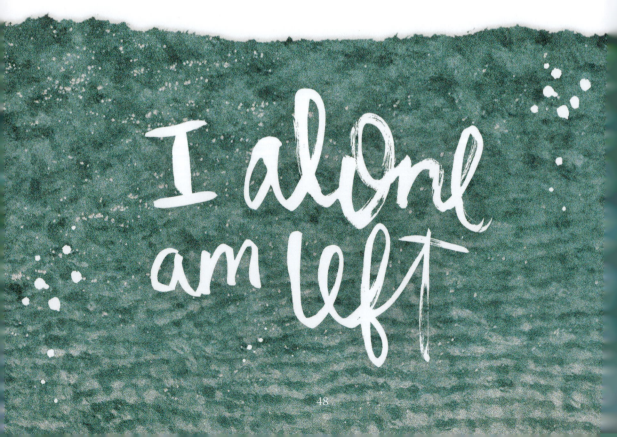

I alone am left

PROMPT

Has there been a time, perhaps during a spiritual retreat, when you had the opportunity to steal away from your day-to-day responsibilities and meet with God? If so, write about that experience below. If not, take time to brainstorm some ways you might make space for God.

DIG DEEPER

Exodus 19:1–9
Exodus 24:12–18
Romans 11:1–6

DAY 8

Home to Tarsus

As Saul stood on the deck of the ship carrying him away from Israel and back home to Tarsus, the bustling city of Caesarea Maritima slowly receded from view.

Caesarea Maritima was a stunning feat of engineering. The homes and shops of the common people rested farthest inland. Far grander structures sat nearer to the coast. A towering Roman theater anchored one end of the city, and Herod the Great's luxurious palace, built around a huge pool cut out of the bedrock, jutted out into the Mediterranean Sea.

The city also had soaring temples, bathhouses, and a sewer system, but the true wonder of Caesarea Maritima was the man-made harbor, where a lighthouse burned twenty-four hours a day.

Now Saul was leaving it all behind. After returning from Sinai, he had gone to Jerusalem to meet with other followers of Jesus, but the visit had been complicated. When Saul, seemingly oblivious to just how dangerous Jerusalem had become for the followers of Christ, brashly began to argue publicly that Jesus was the Messiah, his boldness had not only put his own life in danger, but it also put the other apostles at greater risk. So the leaders of the church in Jerusalem snatched Saul out of harm's way and sent him home, where he could, hopefully, stay out of trouble.

Back in Tarsus, ten quiet years slipped by as Saul navigated his very Roman world. He listened to philosophers debate the meaning of life and watched as the throngs streamed toward pagan temples. As he did business with and lived alongside his Gentile neighbors, Saul witnessed all the ways human beings demean, injure, and mistreat each other when they worship idols instead of the one true God.

Day after long day, Saul bent over his tentmaker's bench, practicing his trade, but as his needle passed in and out of the leather, his mind was busy weaving the reality of Jesus the Messiah into the Scriptures hidden in his mind and heart.

Saul waited and waited as days slipped into months, and months piled up into years.

What would the future bring? Would God open the door for Saul to fulfill the ministry to which He had called him? Had God forgotten he was there in his workshop, working and waiting?

But God had not forgotten. He was at work.

There in the mundane rhythms of each day, God was preparing Saul for his future ministry. What seemed from the outside as wasted years, was the training ground for all that would come.

Saul worked, pondered, and prayed. He waited at the threshold of the next chapter in his life as, in the silence and stillness, God equipped him for his mission.

SCRIPTURE READING

Read the passage below to discover the firsthand account of what happened in Jerusalem that prompted the apostles to send Saul back home to Tarsus, where he would spend years waiting for God to open the door for his ministry.

Acts 9:19–30 NRSV

For several days he was with the disciples in Damascus, and immediately he began to proclaim Jesus in the synagogues, saying, "He is the Son of God." All who heard him were amazed and said, "Is not this the man who made havoc in Jerusalem among those who invoked this name? And has he not come here for the purpose of bringing them bound before the chief priests?" Saul became increasingly more powerful and confounded the Jews who lived in Damascus by proving that Jesus was the Messiah.

After some time had passed, the Jews plotted to kill him, but their plot became known to Saul. They were watching the gates day and night so that they might kill him; but his disciples took him by night and let him down through an opening in the wall, lowering him in a basket.

When he had come to Jerusalem, he attempted to join the disciples; and they were all afraid of him, for they did not believe that he was a disciple. But Barnabas took him, brought him to the apostles, and described for them how on the road he had seen the Lord, who had spoken to him, and how in Damascus he had spoken boldly in the name of Jesus. So he went in and out among them in Jerusalem, speaking boldly in the name of the Lord. He spoke and argued with the Hellenists; but they were attempting to kill him. When the believers learned of it, they brought him down to Caesarea and sent him off to Tarsus.

LET'S REVIEW

To save Saul's life, the apostles sent him back home to Tarsus. Considering Saul's personality, including the fact that he never shied away from an argument, what conflicts do you imagine arose when he was back home, living with his devout Pharisaical family? Can you relate?

Saul spends approximately the next ten years in Tarsus. On the surface, it might have appeared that he was stuck in limbo, but God was actively preparing him for his ministry.

According to our narrative today, what were some of the things God was likely doing in Saul's mind and heart to equip him for ministry to the Gentiles?

The only time Saul mentions this season in Tarsus is in II Corinthians 12:7–10. He says he was given "a thorn in the flesh" during this time to keep him from becoming arrogant.

What differences do you see between young Saul and the man he became during his years of waiting in Tarsus?

APPLICATION

During his decade in Tarsus, Saul was in a "liminal space." The word *liminal* comes from the Latin word *limen*, which means "threshold." Liminal spaces are "in between" seasons of life in which God teaches and prepares us for what He has in store for us.

Liminal spaces are rarely, if ever, comfortable places. They are marked by uncertainty and instability. In liminal spaces, we often find ourselves wondering what the future holds for us. We get frustrated with the drudgery of waiting.

It feels like we are in limbo.

There is a huge difference between being stuck in limbo and inhabiting a liminal space. The term *limbo* originated in the thirteenth century within the Roman Catholic Church. It was believed to be the border of hell.

The meaning of the word evolved over time as words do. The Advanced English Dictionary defines *limbo* as "an imaginary place for lost or neglected things; *the state of being disregarded or forgotten*" (emphasis added).

In limbo, one is lost in the dark, abandoned. In a liminal space, the tender eye of God never leaves us. It is a holy place from which we emerge changed, healthy, and whole.

No matter how deeply the shadows have fallen in our lives or how long and wearisome the wait, God never forgets us. In those seasons of waiting, He is faithfully preparing us for all that is to come.

God is preparing us

PROMPT

We all experience frustrating seasons of waiting from time to time. Think back to one of these periods in your life. What did you learn? How did you grow?

DIG DEEPER

Romans 8:18–28
Philippians 1:3–6
Psalm 27:13–14

DAY 9

To Antioch

For ten years, Saul's life moved in a familiar orbit. He made tents and went to the synagogue. He spent time with family and neighbors. He studied and prayed.

Saul worked, worshiped, and waited as God threaded Jesus through every inch of his life, making something new.

Then the day came when Saul's season of quiet preparation for ministry ended as abruptly as it had begun.

The door to his tentmaker's shop swung open, but when Saul looked up to greet the next customer, he found an old friend instead. Barnabas stood there smiling. A few more wrinkles were etched into his face, but he had the same kind eyes.

Barnabas was a nickname. His given name was Joseph, but his relentless efforts to lift others up prompted the apostles in Jerusalem to lovingly call him Barnabas, the son of encouragement.

Saul had once been the recipient of Barnabas' kindness. When he'd tried to join the apostles in Jerusalem, he found they wouldn't meet with him out of fear of his past persecution of the church. When Barnabas learned of their rejection, he went looking for Saul, took him back to the apostles, and advocated for him. Because of Barnabas, they gave Saul a chance.

Now Barnabas had come looking for Saul again, this time to escort him out of his season of waiting and into his ministry.

Barnabas was fresh from Antioch with exciting news. God was doing something brand new there. The good news of Jesus the Messiah had overflowed from the synagogues into the streets, sweeping Gentiles into the river of God's grace, and now they were worshiping Jesus alongside their Jewish brothers and sisters. God was forming a new family, and you didn't have to be a descendant of Abraham to be a part of it. All that mattered was whether you trusted in Jesus.

Some in the church at Jerusalem had been alarmed at the news. The line between Jew and Gentile had always been fixed, unmovable, much like the division between men and women, masters and slaves.

But Barnabas had found the Spirit of God alive and active in this new community of faith. He was overjoyed, but quickly realized that if they were going to remain united in their love of God and each other in a world that pressured them to maintain the old divisions, they not only needed a firm foundation in the Scriptures but also someone who could help them understand how Jesus both fit into and fulfilled them. Saul, with his deep understanding of God's Word and years of pondering the mystery of Jesus the Messiah, was the perfect candidate.

So Saul gathered his tentmakers' tools, said bittersweet goodbyes to the people he loved, and went with Barnabas to Syrian Antioch, a diverse, booming city of 250 thousand. There he found a small group of Jesus followers who were rejecting every customary division to find unity in the Messiah.

Saul lived alongside them. He taught them, loved them, and learned from them. Together, they nurtured the seedbed of the early church, and the fruit it bore changed the world forever.

SCRIPTURE READING

While Saul waited for ten long years in Tarsus, God was not only preparing him for ministry, but He was also preparing the ministry for Saul. Read the Scripture below to find out how the early church and Saul's ministry were founded.

Acts 11:19–26 NRSV

Now those who were scattered because of the persecution that took place over Stephen traveled as far as Phoenicia, Cyprus, and Antioch, and they spoke the word to no one except Jews. But among them were some men of Cyprus and Cyrene who, on coming to Antioch, spoke to the Hellenists also, proclaiming the Lord Jesus. The hand of the Lord was with them, and a great number became believers and turned to the Lord. News of this came to the ears of the church in Jerusalem, and they sent Barnabas to Antioch. When he came and saw the grace of God, he rejoiced, and he exhorted them all to remain faithful to the Lord with steadfast devotion; for he was a good man, full of the Holy Spirit and of faith. And a great many people were brought to the Lord. Then Barnabas went to Tarsus to look for Saul, and when he had found him, he brought him to Antioch. So it was that for an entire year they met with the church and taught a great many people, and it was in Antioch that the disciples were first called "Christians."

LET'S REVIEW

Barnabas, the son of encouragement, is a wonderful example of how each of us can use our unique gifts to help build the kingdom of God.

How do you think Saul's ministry would have been affected if Barnabas had not fully lived into his gift of encouragement?

The Gentiles in the new church at Syrian Antioch were eager to follow Jesus, but Barnabas realized they had a serious vulnerability—they knew nothing of the Scriptures their Jewish brothers and sisters had studied their whole lives. Barnabas knew they needed a solid foundation of God's Word.

What verse or passage of Scripture has most helped you grow in your faith?

Our Scripture today tells us that the disciples were first called "Christians" at Syrian Antioch. The word Christian means "little Christ." Radical unity is one of the hallmarks of what it means to follow Jesus.

Do you think the modern church is doing a good job when it comes to unity? Why or why not?

APPLICATION

Sinful humans find great comfort in "us versus them." It gives us something to cling to that allows us to feel more valuable, more worthy than our neighbors. Jesus has a different standard.

Jesus was a servant to all, and He calls us to humbly love and serve each other. Jesus submitted to death on the cross so that we might be saved, and He asks us to take up our own "cross," to die to self and follow Him.

There is no room for hierarchy in the kingdom of God. Jesus alone is Lord. The rest of us stand on level ground at the foot of the cross. This kind of unity and equality will forever offend and threaten those who find their worth in their position.

Saul spent his ministry tirelessly challenging the young church to live up to this standard. His firm belief that Jesus was Lord and that His death on the cross made a way for us to live in unity got him in trouble everywhere he went, but he never shied away from proclaiming the truth of the Gospel.

It takes courage to truly live as a Christ-follower—courage to confront our own biases and courage to ensure that everyone has a seat at God's table. But God has called us to be people of love and courage. In this way, we proclaim the good news of Jesus, the Messiah, until He returns.

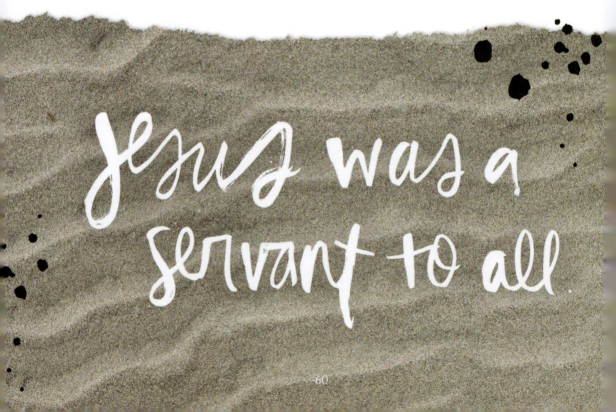

Jesus was a servant to all

PROMPT

Barnabas, the encourager, never hesitated to use his influence and position to lift others. Write about a time when someone encouraged you and how it impacted your life. Then take some time to pray, asking God whom you might encourage today.

DIG DEEPER

I Corinthians 12:12–13
Matthew 13:1–9
Mark 9:33–37

DAY 10

A Gift for Jerusalem

It began with a prophecy.

Agabus, a prophet from Jerusalem, was visiting Saul, Barnabas, and the church at Syrian Antioch. Filled with the Spirit of God, he stood up in the room of worshipers and made his proclamation.

A severe famine was coming. Its crushing reach would be long and wide. No country in the Mediterranean world would be spared.

A gasp of alarm echoed throughout the room, followed by the buzz of chatter as everyone began to process the looming crisis and make plans on how to prepare.

Their primary concern, however, was not for their own future needs. Instead, they were focused on how they could send assistance to the church in Jerusalem.

Syrian Antioch was a major commercial center. A famine would certainly cause distress as the price of grain skyrocketed, but it would be nothing compared to the suffering in Jerusalem. Not only would grain be more expensive there, for merchants had to travel to sell the wares, but the believers in Jerusalem were already suffering financially. During the early days after Christ's resurrection, many of them had sold all they owned in expectation that the Messiah's return was imminent, but He had yet to return, and in His absence the church in Jerusalem had also suffered persecution. They were among the poorest of the poor.

The church in Antioch pooled their resources and then sent Saul, Barnabas, and Titus, a young Gentile follower of Christ, to Jerusalem to deliver the gift.

The three men gathered their supplies for the three-hundred-mile trip and set off. For more than two weeks, they traveled south along the Mediterranean coast, over mountains, and across rivers until they reached Jerusalem.

The temple rose majestically in the center of the city with magnificent mansions nestled around its flanks. But the believers in Jerusalem didn't live among the ease and beauty of the wealthy. Their modest homes were in the poorest section of town.

When Saul, Barnabas, and Titus arrived with their gift, the believers were overjoyed, but as they spent time with their brothers from Antioch, a disturbing truth became clear—Titus was an "unclean," uncircumcised Gentile.

The Jewish believers, accustomed to their ancestral traditions surrounding purity, recoiled from the young man, refusing to share meals with him unless he underwent circumcision according to Jewish law.

Saul and Barnabas were outraged, and Saul wasted no time in confronting them. Jesus, he argued, had launched a new creation through His sacrifice on the cross. In doing so, He had established a new covenant. Since this covenant was not built around the law but a relationship with the Messiah, it was open to everyone. Titus, as a Gentile, was no longer unclean because Jesus' sacrifice had made him clean once and for all.

If, Saul reasoned, they allowed their Jewish brothers to force the requirements of the law onto Titus, it was like dragging him into slavery.

The leaders of the church in Jerusalem, Peter, James, and John, agreed, and Titus was spared.

But the issue was far from dead. It was only sleeping, and before long, it would rise again with such vengeance that it would threaten the very existence of the early church.

SCRIPTURE READING

Read the two accounts below to learn about the gift to Jerusalem and the conflict that surrounded it.

Luke's Account | Acts 11:27–30 NRSV

At that time prophets came down from Jerusalem to Antioch. One of them named Agabus stood up and predicted by the Spirit that there would be a severe famine over all the world; and this took place during the reign of Claudius. The disciples determined that according to their ability, each would send relief to the believer living in Judea; this they did, sending it to the elders by Barnabas and Saul.

Saul's Firsthand Account | Galatians 2:1–10 NRSV

Then after fourteen years I went up again to Jerusalem with Barnabas, taking Titus along with me. I went up in response to a revelation. Then I laid before them (though only in a private meeting with the acknowledged leaders) the gospel that I proclaim among the Gentiles, in order to make sure that I was not running, or had not run, in vain. But even Titus, who was with me, was not compelled to be circumcised, though he was a Greek. But because of false believers secretly brought in, who slipped in to spy on the freedom we have in Christ Jesus, so that they might enslave us—we did not submit to them even for a moment, so that the truth of the gospel might always remain with you. And from those who were supposed to be acknowledged leaders (what they actually were makes no difference to me; God shows no partiality)—those leaders contributed nothing to me. On the contrary, when they saw that I had been entrusted with the gospel for the uncircumcised, just as Peter had been entrusted with the gospel for the circumcised (for He who worked through Peter making him an apostle to the circumcised also worked through me in sending me to the Gentiles), and when James and Cephas and John, who were acknowledged pillars, recognized the grace that had been given to me, they gave to Barnabas and me the right hand of fellowship, agreeing that we should go to the Gentiles and they to the circumcised. They asked only one thing, that we remember the poor, which was actually what I was eager to do.

Most of us feel the impulse to defensively protect our resources when we are faced with a crisis, but this wasn't what the believers at Syrian Antioch did.

Think back to a time when you were in crisis but learned of the greater needs of others. How did you respond?

The church in Jerusalem was comprised of Jewish believers, among them Jesus' disciples, who still carefully followed the Torah. The concept of God's new family of both Jews and Gentiles had yet to reach the Holy City, so they refused to welcome Titus into their fellowship, unless he was circumcised.

When someone different from you walks into church on Sunday morning, how do you react? Do you want them to clean themselves up before coming to church, or do you welcome them as they are? Why?

When Saul speaks of the Jewish believers' attempts to force the restrictions and requirements of the law onto Gentile followers of Christ, he uses the word enslave. *How are we "enslaved" when we attempt to live sinlessly apart from dependence on the sacrifice of Jesus and empowerment from the Holy Spirit?*

APPLICATION

Today's reading is the story of two groups of believers. It is also the story of God's abundance and man's fear of scarcity.

One group of Christ-followers so believed in God's abundance that they trusted He would meet their needs in the face of an impending famine. From that place of security, they gave freely of their financial resources to their brothers and sisters in Jerusalem.

The other group, however, couldn't imagine a grace big enough, lavish enough, or abundant enough, to cover the Gentiles, who had once been outside of the family of God. As a result, they excluded one of the men who had traveled hundreds of miles to bring them help in their time of need.

From the moment Adam and Eve rebelled against God in the garden of Eden, the fear of scarcity has driven us to live selfishly rather than generously. God, however, is a God of abundance, and as His children we live—and give—from a place of abundance. This generosity, however, is not limited to material things. It also means offering grace, mercy, and acceptance freely.

The key to all this is the presence of the Spirit of God in our lives. When we trust the Spirit's leading, our fears are silenced, and we find ourselves more able and willing to lower our walls of self-protection and give generously.

god of abundance

PROMPT

Where in your life do you fear scarcity today? Write down your needs for today, and then ask God to help you trust that all you need is in His loving hands.

DIG DEEPER

Psalm 36:7–9
Psalm 112:1–5
II Corinthians 9:6–8

DAY 11

The Slavery of Idolatry in Lystra

The time had come to leave Syrian Antioch and spread the good news of Jesus the Messiah far and wide. Paul, Barnabas, and Barnabas' nephew John Mark made their way to the closest port, hopped on a ship, and headed for Cyprus. After that, it was back on another ship to head north to Perga. At this point, John Mark left the group to return to Jerusalem while Paul and Barnabas journeyed inland to Pisidian Antioch and then east across the mountains and into Syria.

From there, they visited Iconium before coming to Lystra.

In each city, their pattern was the same: They began by proclaiming the Messiah in the synagogues to the Jews and then turned their attention to the Gentiles. In Lystra, that's when everything got out of hand.

As Paul stood teaching, a man in the crowd caught his eye. He sat on the ground. Both feet were twisted grotesquely, condemning him to a life of begging and suffering.

But his eyes. There was something about his eyes. They were locked onto Paul's face with a mixture of earnest desperation and hope. This man's body was broken, but his faith was strong.

Filled with the liberating, restoring Spirit of God, Paul couldn't turn away. He stopped in the middle of his discourse and commanded the man to stand. Immediately, bones and tendons marred from birth slipped into place. Then the man leapt from his mat and walked.

The crowd went crazy.

Much to Paul and Barnabas' horror, however, the citizens of Lystra didn't understand that they had just witnessed Jesus' resurrection power breaking through a wounded creation to restore a man's life. They assumed their gods, Zeus and his messenger, Hermes, had finally shown up to walk among them.

The crowd began shouting, joyfully announcing their arrival. A priest of Zeus arrived with oxen and garlands, prepared to sacrifice to the "gods." The crowd sang, chanted, and danced.

Paul and Barnabas rushed into the crowd, desperate to stop the pagan celebration. The two men knew the sin of idolatry was deadly. From the time Paul and Barnabas were small boys, they had heard the stories of how their ancestors turned from the one true God, who brought them out of Egypt, to worship false gods. They learned how Israel, doubting God's provision, turned to the Canaanite fertility god, Baal—who was often depicted with a bolt of lightning in one hand and wheat in the other—to ensure the rains fell on their crops at just the right time.

Now another misguided people was eager to appease another false god with a thunderbolt in his hand. According to their pagan traditions, Zeus, the god of weather, held the power to send the rains or withhold them. Hermes was his messenger.

Idolatry always offers up the same, sweet lie: If only you can make the gods happy, offer the right sacrifice, you can manipulate them into doing what you want.

But God wants all people to trust Him for provision—which He gives lovingly, abundantly, with no strings attached.

He wants them to be free.

Slowly the roar of the crowd quieted, but before Paul and Barnabas had finished pointing them back to the one true God, a new threat arrived. Some Jews who had heard their message of the Messiah and rejected it entered the mix. And they were out for blood.

Vengefully, they stirred the crowd once again, manipulating them to turn on the men who, only a few minutes before, they had esteemed as deities. The mob seized Paul, dragged him outside the city, stoned him, and left him for dead.

Once the crowd dispersed, Paul's anxious friends gathered around him to find, to their amazement, that he was still breathing. After a moment, he struggled to his feet, bruised and bloody, but very much alive.

God wasn't finished with His servant yet. The kingdom of God had come through Jesus' work on the cross. He is the God of the thunder and the rain, the God who came to set all people free.

Paul still had work to do, to proclaim the good news that the Messiah had come. And the world was waiting.

SCRIPTURE READING

Read the Scripture below for Luke's account of Paul and Barnabas' dramatic visit to Lystra.

Acts 14:8–20 NIV

In Lystra there sat a man who was lame. He had been that way from birth and had never walked. He listened to Paul as he was speaking. Paul looked directly at him, saw that he had faith to be healed and called out, "Stand up on your feet!" At that, the man jumped up and began to walk.

When the crowd saw what Paul had done, they shouted in the Lycaonian language, "The gods have come down to us in human form!" Barnabas they called Zeus, and Paul they called Hermes because he was the chief speaker. The priest of Zeus, whose temple was just outside the city, brought bulls and wreaths to the city gates because he and the crowd wanted to offer sacrifices to them.

But when the apostles Barnabas and Paul heard of this, they tore their clothes and rushed out into the crowd, shouting: "Friends, why are you doing this? We too are only human, like you. We are bringing you good news, telling you to turn from these worthless things to the living God, who made the heavens and the earth and the sea and everything in them. In the past, He let all nations go their own way. Yet He has not left Himself without testimony: He has shown kindness by giving you rain from heaven and crops in their seasons; He provides you with plenty of food and fills your hearts with joy." Even with these words, they had difficulty keeping the crowd from sacrificing to them.

Then some Jews came from Antioch and Iconium and won the crowd over. They stoned Paul and dragged him outside the city, thinking he was dead. But after the disciples had gathered around him, he got up and went back into the city. The next day he and Barnabas left for Derbe.

In the world of the Bible, life depended heavily upon crops receiving rain and dew at the proper times, in the proper amount. Without them, famine ensued. Fear of crop failure was a big reason people turned to gods they felt had power over the weather.

How do you think fear of not having your needs met makes you vulnerable to placing your trust in something other than God?

When the children of Israel turned to idols to meet their needs instead of the God who had led them out of Egypt, they quickly found themselves in a whole new kind of slavery. How does putting our trust in anything other than the living God enslave us?

One minute the citizens of Lystra were hailing Paul as a god; the next, they stoned him. Somehow, he survived. Even more remarkable, he didn't let the experience slow him down. He simply moved on to the next city to preach the Gospel. What do you think motivated Paul and gave him the courage to keep going?

APPLICATION

The gods were everywhere in the Roman world. Keeping them happy was top priority, not just for the well-being of individuals, but for the whole community. Anyone who didn't fall in line was considered dangerous because they put everyone at risk of suffering the gods' wrath. As Paul came of age and began his ministry, a new god was intentionally added to the many others—Caesar himself. After all, what better way to keep a people under a ruler's thumb than to convince them that he was not just the emperor, but also a god?

Any time we elevate something or someone other than God to a place of authority in our lives, we are setting ourselves up for suffering and oppression. Only the true God, the merciful, kind Creator of heaven and earth, can be trusted to govern our lives in a way that leads us to freedom and abundance.

The Old Testament tells us that when the children of Israel turned to idolatry, they left the safety of a faithful God who provided for them, and found themselves trapped, constantly trying to appease and manipulate a false god, Baal, so he would provide the dew and the rain.

This plunged them into the slavery of fear. Were they doing enough to keep their false god happy? What sacrifice did he require? Would he, fickle as he was, send the rain on their crops when they needed it or not?

These manipulations resulted in the dehumanization and wounding of every person in the scenario. Jeremiah 19:4–5 records for us God's heartbreaking cry over His children's idolatry and the devastation it brought them:

> The people have forsaken Me, and have profaned this place by making offerings in it to other gods whom neither they nor their ancestors nor the kings of Judah have known, and because they have filled this place with the blood of the innocent, and gone on building the high places of Baal to burn their children in the fire as burnt offerings to Baal, which I did not command or decree, nor did it enter My mind. (NRSV)

The children of Israel sacrificed their own children by fire to keep Baal happy, whereas Jesus gave Himself over to the fires of suffering and death that we might live.

We all worship someone or something.

Whom will you choose?

fully devoted to you.

PROMPT

Most of us struggle to keep God at the center of our lives. Have you ever replaced God with someone or something else? If so, write about that experience below. When we do this, it is tempting to run from Him in our shame. His love, however, is always greater than our weaknesses and failures. Receive His forgiveness today and ask Him to give you a heart that is fully devoted to Him.

DIG DEEPER

II Kings 17:7–17
Jeremiah 2:11–12
Leviticus 26:1–5

DAY 12

The Law and the Cross

The moment Peter and Barnabas turned their backs on the Gentile believers in Antioch would remain seared in Paul's memory forever.

Peter had come to Antioch with open arms for his Gentile brothers and sisters after receiving a vision from the Lord declaring that the dividing lines of clean and unclean had been wiped away in the Messiah. He lived alongside them, worshiped with them, and even shared their meals—only to lose his courage and go back on what he knew to be right and true when it mattered most.

This would have been deeply hurtful from anyone, but since Peter was well-respected as one of the pillars of the young church, men who had known the Messiah during His earthly ministry, it was especially devastating.

Peter's choices, wise or unwise, had a far wider impact than on his life alone. When he faltered under pressure from Jewish believers from Jerusalem, who insisted that the Gentiles had to conform to the law, including circumcision, others followed his lead.

Even Barnabas.

Barnabas, who had first embraced the Gentile believers at Antioch.

Barnabas, who had worked alongside Paul for so long.

Barnabas, who had traveled hundreds of miles with Paul, rejoiced with him, and *suffered* with him.

Even Barnabas turned away.

It was deeply hurtful, but it was also incredibly dangerous. The very essence of the Gospel was at stake.

Paul knew that he had to do something decisive and do it quickly. He leveled a steely gaze at Peter, in front of everyone, and held nothing back. He called him out for asking his Gentile brothers and sisters to submit to the law when he, a Jew, had not even been doing so in his time with them. Peter had embraced his own freedom in Christ alongside the Gentile believers, only to pretend otherwise when he felt pressure from those who had yet to fully understand and accept the freedom Jesus purchased for them on the cross.

Paul called Peter a hypocrite, someone who was pretending to be something he wasn't for the sake of appearances. After all, Paul argued, if man needed the law to stand justified before God, didn't Jesus die for nothing?

If it was possible to achieve justification through the law, it would have happened long ago. Paul knew that even the most devout Jew—and he had been one of them—was a lawbreaker at some point.

God's grace, given through the crucified Messiah, was the only cure for man's sin.

Paul, who had once been so proud of his own righteousness, had encountered the reality of his own sinfulness on the road to Damascus, and he would never be the same. The man he was before, the man under the law, died that day. He had been crucified with Christ and miraculously raised with Him to walk in new life.

It was a freedom bought at a great price, and Paul would stop at nothing to ensure that everyone, Jew or Gentile, had the opportunity to receive God's lavish gift.

SCRIPTURE READING

In today's reading, Paul refers to Peter by the Aramaic form of his name, Cephas. Read Paul's account of the moment Peter (Cephas) and Barnabas gave in to pressure from some of the Jews from Jerusalem to exclude their Gentile brothers and sisters.

Galatians 2:11–21 NRSV

But when Cephas came to Antioch, I opposed him to his face, because he stood self-condemned; for until certain people came from James, he used to eat with the Gentiles. But after they came, he drew back and kept himself separate for fear of the circumcision faction. And the other Jews joined him in this hypocrisy, so that even Barnabas was led astray by their hypocrisy. But when I saw that they were not acting consistently with the truth of the gospel, I said to Cephas before them all, "If you, though a Jew, live like a Gentile and not like a Jew, how can you compel the Gentiles to live like Jews?"

We ourselves are Jews by birth and not Gentile sinners; yet we know that a person is justified not by the works of the law but through faith in Jesus Christ. And we have come to believe in Christ Jesus, so that we might be justified by faith in Christ, and not by doing the works of the law, because no one will be justified by the works of the law. But if, in our effort to be justified in Christ, we ourselves have been found to be sinners, is Christ then a servant of sin? Certainly not! But if I build up again the very things that I once tore down, then I demonstrate that I am a transgressor. For through the law I died to the law, so that I might live to God. I have been crucified with Christ; and it is no longer I who live, but it is Christ who lives in me. And the life I now live in the flesh I live by faith in the Son of God, who loved me and gave Himself for me. I do not nullify the grace of God; for if justification comes through the law, then Christ died for nothing.

LET'S REVIEW

In the culture of the Bible, a meal was always more than a meal. To sit down to eat with some-one sent a clear message of acceptance. It was the same as calling them a friend. How do you think the Gentile believers felt when Peter, who had previously joined them for meals, suddenly pulled away from them?

More than two thousand years later, it is easy to see how the law-loving Jews from Jerusalem completely missed the point of Jesus' sacrifice on the cross, but Christians today often fall into a similar trap. Our holy living should flow out of our relationship with Christ, not to serve as a means to achieve justification, or righteousness.

Are you trying to keep God's law so He will declare you righteous? How would your life change if you fully embraced the truth that you can do nothing to earn your justification?

Some of us were taught that forgiveness is God's job, but repentance is ours. In Luke 15, Jesus tells a parable about three "lost things": a coin, a sheep, and a lost son. In each story, the one that is lost is utterly dependent on someone else to make it back home. Repentance, Jesus is telling us, is God's work. Our part is simple; We must be willing to be found and carried back home.

Does this definition of repentance *surprise you? Why or why not?*

APPLICATION

In *The Lion, the Witch, and the Wardrobe* by C.S. Lewis, the Christ-figure of the book is Aslan, a massive lion. When the human children make their way into the land of Narnia, where Aslan is king, they encounter two talking beavers who tell them all about Aslan.

One of the children asks if Aslan is "safe." Mr. Beaver is appalled at the thought.

"Safe?" said Mr. Beaver. "Don't you hear what Mrs. Beaver tells you? Who said anything about safe? 'Course he isn't safe. But he's good. He's the King, I tell you."

Moralism is a philosophy that focuses on rule following, as opposed to grace, to achieve justification. Of course, it is impossible to follow the rules so perfectly that we stand blameless before God, but that doesn't stop some of us from trying. Perhaps one of the reasons we prefer moralism to reckless dependence on the mercy of God is that it feels like we have control over something.

The God of the universe, however, is not controllable. He is holy and mighty, infinite and fierce.

He is in no way tame, but He is *good*.

Moralism offers us the sweet temptation of a justification we can achieve for ourselves, but like all the evil one's deceits, there is a steep hidden cost: Moralism doesn't satisfy. It either lures us into the deception of self-righteousness or crushes us under the weight of shame. It enslaves us under the weight of "keeping up appearances," pretending to be something we are not to avoid condemnation.

Only Jesus justifies through His sacrifice on the cross. The work of redemption is His alone. We must be vigilant to resist the temptation to give ourselves too much credit for the process. Our only hope is to fall completely on the grace of Christ.

As Paul would later write in his letter to the Ephesians, we are saved by grace through faith, a gift freely given to us by God (Ephesians 2:8). There is no room for pride or self-righteousness. Our part is to simply receive the gift, to lift our arms to the Father in childlike faith, and to let Him carry us back home

He is good

PROMPT

Take some time to journal about the ways you have tried to achieve righteousness through your own efforts. How did they impact your relationships with God and with others?

DIG DEEPER

Ephesians 2:1–10
Psalm 130:1–8
Acts 10:9–48

DAY 13

Paul's Temper and God's Grace

When the last bitter word had been said, the final argument made, Paul and Barnabas were still in the same room, but there was a scorched wasteland between them where friendship had once bloomed.

Memories hung between the two men in the silence:

> The moment Barnabas showed up in Tarsus to escort Paul out of ten long years of waiting and into his ministry . . .

> The expectant, joyful faces of the believers in Antioch when the two men arrived to teach them and live among them . . .

> The way the two men strengthened and comforted each other as they endured imprisonment, floggings, beatings, and raging mobs . . .

During the early days after Paul's conversion, when he tried to join the apostles in Jerusalem only to experience their rejection, it was Barnabas, the lover of second chances, who vouched for him with the apostles. Barnabas made a way for Paul, the outcast, to have a seat at the table of fellowship.

But when Barnabas urged Paul to give John Mark a second chance, the opportunity to prove himself after he had abandoned their ministry in Perga, Paul was unwilling to offer the young man the same grace he had once received.

Barnabas looked across the room at Paul to find his eyes angry, his jaw set.

How could he?

Barnabas' heart was broken. He gathered his things, retrieved John Mark, and prepared to sail to Cyprus. It was time to go home.

SCRIPTURE READING

Read the Scriptures below for Luke's account of the disagreement that ended Paul and Barnabas' partnership in the Gospel.

Acts 13:13 NRSV

Then Paul and his companions set sail from Paphos and came to Perga in Pamphylia. John, however, left them and returned to Jerusalem.

Acts 15:36–39 NRSV

After some days Paul said to Barnabas, "Come, let us return and visit the believers in every city where we proclaimed the word of the Lord and see how they are doing." Barnabas wanted to take with them John called Mark. But Paul decided not to take with them one who had deserted them in Pamphylia and had not accompanied them in the work. The disagreement became so sharp that they parted company; Barnabas took Mark with him and sailed away to Cyprus.

LET'S REVIEW

What did Paul tell Barnabas was the purpose of his second missionary journey when he asked Barnabas to join him?

Why didn't Paul want to take John Mark along with them?

Paul's boldness was a gift he needed to proclaim the Gospel in dangerous and difficult situations. This time, however, his fiery personality harmed instead of helped.

Think about your strengths. How do they have the potential to harm if you fail to keep them in submission to God?

APPLICATION

John Mark's failings were all too clear to Paul, but Paul, it seems, was a bit blind to some of his own, particularly his unbridled temper.

Paul believed in reconciliation. He literally put his skin on the line to reconcile Jews and Gentiles to each other, and all men to God.

In this incident, however, his flesh got the best of him. He acted out of his anger instead of love, and in doing so, his friendship with Barnabas was fractured beyond repair. Scripture gives no indication that they ever reconciled.

Sometimes we shy away from facing our sin honestly because we fear shame and condemnation. It helps to remember that Jesus has compassion on us in our sin. He gave His life so that we might have forgiveness. As Isaiah 53:5 says,

> But He was wounded for our transgressions,
> crushed for our iniquities;
> upon Him was the punishment that made us whole,
> and by His bruises we are healed. (NRSV)

Sin is a wound. Jesus wants to heal it so that we might have abundant life.

In the Lord's Prayer, we pray, "forgive us our sins as we forgive those who sin against us." It is far more difficult to truly forgive others if we have not first faced our own failings and humbly received God's forgiveness. The two go hand in hand.

Claiming grace without facing our sin fails to open our hearts to God's healing touch. Facing our sin apart from the security found in God's forgiveness leaves us defeated and broken.

We can't heal what we can't face, and we can't face that which we do not trust God to heal.

covered by God's grace

PROMPT

Is there a sin in your life that you struggle with repeatedly? In the space below, write down these words of forgiveness written by Paul: "There is therefore now no condemnation for those who are in Christ Jesus" (Romans 8:1 NRSV). And journal about what this Scripture means to you.

You are covered by God's grace. He longs to heal you. Lay it all at His feet.

DIG DEEPER

Hebrews 12:1–2
I John 5:1–10
I Timothy 1:12–17

DAY 14

The Shadow of God's Silence

Paul opened his eyes in the half light, his sleeping mat beneath him and a thatched roof overhead, to find that just as the misty world of his dreams surrendered to the hard, clear reality of the morning, so one season of his life was fading away, another to take its place.

Barnabas, Paul's friend and partner in ministry for so many years, was gone.

Paul sat up and rubbed his eyes as his thoughts buzzed like a swarm of angry bees. What would life and ministry be like without Barnabas by his side?

He would need a new partner, of course, and Silas seemed like the best choice. Together, the two men would set out to visit the churches he and Barnabas had planted to see how they were doing before heading east to preach the Gospel in the great city of Ephesus.

Yes, to Asia he and Silas would go.

It would be difficult to say goodbye to the believers at Antioch, and awkward to explain Barnabas' sudden absence, but it felt good to have a plan.

But Paul was about to learn that sometimes what seems like a good plan to us isn't on God's agenda at all.

At first, everything seemed to be going well. Paul and Silas headed north, with a smooth Roman road beneath their feet and a cool breeze blowing off the beautiful blue Mediterranean Sea to their left. A day's journey brought them to the city of Issus, where they turned east and journeyed for two more days before arriving in Paul's hometown of Tarsus.

After resting and gathering supplies, Paul and Silas journeyed toward the daunting Tarsus Mountains. After a long day of travel, the two men dismounted from their donkeys to rest for the night before traversing the perilous Cilician Gates, a narrow gorge carved through the mountains by eons of raging water from the river at its base.

Once the two men safely made it to the other side of the mountains, they turned to the east and traveled for three more days, passing through Derbe before arriving in Lystra.

Paul and Silas not only enjoyed their time with the church there, but they also picked up a new assistant, Timothy! Spirits were high as the three men prepared to move on to the most exciting stage of their journey. It was time to go into Asia. Ephesus was waiting!

But it was not to be. At just the moment when it seemed everything was falling into place, God threw a cloak of darkness and confusion over it all. The word from the Lord was clear: Paul and his companions were forbidden to go into Ephesus.

There was no explanation. No direction for what to do next. There was only God's no, and the the deafening silence that followed.

The men evaluated their options and decided to head north. After hundreds of miles of grueling travel, they forded the Sangarius River. With relief, it seemed as if they were back on track. Soon, they would arrive at Bythnia, where they would share the good news of the Gospel.

But once more, God clearly told them no before retreating into silence once again.

With few options remaining, the group turned east for another long, exhausting stretch of travel. This time, they followed the coast of the Marmara Sea before finally arriving in the colossal city of Troas.

They were sore, exhausted, and had little to show for their efforts other than the unyielding, cold shadow of God's silence.

SCRIPTURE READING

Read the passage below to hear the scriptural account of Paul's strange, and at times divinely hindered, second missionary journey.

Acts 15:40–16:8 NRSV

But Paul chose Silas and set out, the believers commending him to the grace of the Lord. He went through Syria and Cilicia, strengthening the churches.

Paul went on also to Derbe and to Lystra, where there was a disciple named Timothy, the son of a Jewish woman who was a believer; but his father was a Greek. He was well spoken of by the believers in Lystra and Iconium. Paul wanted Timothy to accompany him; and he took him and had him circumcised because of the Jews who were in those places, for they all knew that his father was a Greek. As they went from town to town, they delivered to them for observance the decisions that had been reached by the apostles and elders who were in Jerusalem. So the churches were strengthened in the faith and increased in numbers daily.

They went through the region of Phrygia and Galatia, having been forbidden by the Holy Spirit to speak the word in Asia. When they had come opposite Mysia, they attempted to go into Bithynia, but the Spirit of Jesus did not allow them; so, passing by Mysia, they went down to Troas.

LET'S REVIEW

It is safe to say that Paul didn't handle the situation with Barnabas and John Mark very well. How do you think God might have used this long, frustrating trip, and His silence along the way, to give Paul time to think about his choices?

Paul seemed to have a good plan for where he wanted to go to preach the Gospel next, but God said no. When God tells you no and it doesn't make sense to you, how do you handle it?

When you experience God's silence, it is easy to feel like something is wrong with you, but saints throughout history have endured the same thing. The psalmist once prayed, "O God, do not remain silent; do not turn a deaf ear, do not stand aloof, O God" (Psalm 83:1 NIV). Periods of God's silence are part of the human experience. You are not alone in that struggle.

Have you ever experienced God's silence? What were you feeling during that time? What did you learn?

APPLICATION

Most of us experience frustrating periods in our lives when God seems silent. These times are never easy. We pray, desperately pleading for direction, wisdom, or words of comfort only to find that God seems to have skipped out on the conversation without even telling us where He was going.

The psalmist never lets God off the hook for this. He gets downright pushy about the issue. He shouts his protest to heaven, demanding God reengage with him. Over and over, the psalmist brazenly insists that God stop the silent treatment and answer him.

Sometimes God is silent because, like Paul, we need a "holy time-out" to give us a chance to compose ourselves, think about our choices, and correct course, but this isn't always the reason.

Sometimes it seems like the shadow of His silence falls over us through no fault of our own, and just when we need Him most.

Whatever the reason for God's silence, it is never easy. It helps to remember that even when we can't feel Him or hear Him, He has promised never to leave us. God enters into our suffering and bears witness to it. He draws near, redeeming our mistakes and our wounds so that He always has the last word.

Are you under the shadow of God's silence today? If so, hang on. God is there, and you *will* get to the place that you can hear Him again. In the meantime, take a cue from the psalmist—press in. Don't hold back. Get pushy with God in prayer. Not only can He handle it, He also welcomes it. God is honored when, like the persistent widow in Luke 18, we just keep knocking at the door of heaven until He answers.

He loves you. He is there even when you can't feel His presence or hear His voice.

Don't be afraid of the silence. God is still near.

god is near

PROMPT

Have you ever experienced a frustrating season of God's silence? If so, write a prayer talking to God about this season and then list three good things that God brought out of that time in your life.

DIG DEEPER

Luke 18:1–8
Psalm 28
Psalm 35

DAY 15

Uncontainable Power

In the darkest hour of the night, when all the world was asleep, God broke His silence.

Paul received a vision from God of a man from Macedonia pleading with him for help. His aimless wanderings had come to an end at last.

Morning light brought a flurry of activity for Paul and his friends. Supplies were purchased and passage across the Aegean Sea secured. Soon, the men were on a ship's deck, the swell of the sea beneath their feet and the salty breeze on their skin. They were headed for Samothrace, a beautiful island with a soaring mountain at its center surrounded by a crystal-clear, vibrant blue sea. After a night's rest on Samothrace, they boarded another ship heading farther north, where they docked at Neapolis before making the short journey by land to the walled city of Philippi.

There were too few Jews in Philippi to support a synagogue, but Paul and his friends discovered a small group of women who met for prayer down by the river. Each Sabbath,

Paul and the other men walked to the river's edge to meet with them to share the good news of the Messiah.

Each time, they were followed by a slave girl possessed by a demon who loudly proclaimed that they were servants of the Most High God who had come to show the residents of Philippi the way of salvation.

The girl, as all slaves in the Roman world, had no rights. She was property, the same as a pair of sandals or a clay pot, with which her owners were free to do with whatever they chose. Her value was not in her humanity, but rather in the income she brought her masters through fortune-telling, which was empowered by the demon who ruled her mind and heart.

This poor slave, utterly bound by her human masters externally *and* by the dark forces that held her captive internally, was pointing the citizens of Philippi to freedom.

Unfortunately, in doing so, she was drawing unwelcome attention to Paul and his friends. Finally, the day came when Paul's short fuse burned out. He turned to her and, in the name of Jesus, commanded the demon to leave her. The evil spirit immediately obeyed.

The girl's eyes cleared as sweet freedom seeped into every corner of her being. Her body remained the property of cruel and unjust men, but her soul was a slave no more.

It was a freedom that came at a high price for everyone involved. Her owners lost the source of their income. The vulnerable girl was thrust into the precarious position of a slave who no longer held any value. Paul and his friends fell in the slave owners' crosshairs because they were to blame.

The infuriated men seized Paul and Silas and dragged them to face the magistrates at the city center, where they accused them of undermining Roman law.

Paul and Silas were publicly stripped, flogged, and then turned over to the prison guard to await their fate. Then the roar of the crowd quieted, and the citizens of Philippi drifted away from the city center and back to their homes and jobs.

The girl was free from the demon that enslaved her. Paul and Silas were in chains.

But the restoring power of Jesus the Messiah was still on the move. It would not, *could not*, ever be contained.

SCRIPTURE READING

Read the scriptural account below of the events in Philippi that led to Paul and Silas's confinement in prison.

Acts 16:9–12, 16–23 NIV

During the night Paul had a vision of a man of Macedonia standing and begging him, "Come over to Macedonia and help us." After Paul had seen the vision, we got ready at once to leave for Macedonia, concluding that God had called us to preach the gospel to them.

From Troas we put out to sea and sailed straight for Samothrace, and the next day we went on to Neapolis. From there we traveled to Philippi, a Roman colony and the leading city of that district of Macedonia. And we stayed there several days....

Once when we were going to the place of prayer, we were met by a female slave who had a spirit by which she predicted the future. She earned a great deal of money for her owners by fortune-telling. She followed Paul and the rest of us, shouting, "These men are servants of the Most High God, who are telling you the way to be saved." She kept this up for many days. Finally Paul became so annoyed that he turned around and said to the spirit, "In the name of Jesus Christ I command you to come out of her!" At that moment the spirit left her.

When her owners realized that their hope of making money was gone, they seized Paul and Silas and dragged them into the marketplace to face the authorities. They brought them before the magistrates and said, "These men are Jews, and are throwing our city into an uproar by advocating customs unlawful for us Romans to accept or practice."

The crowd joined in the attack against Paul and Silas, and the magistrates ordered them to be stripped and beaten with rods. After they had been severely flogged, they were thrown into prison, and the jailer was commanded to guard them carefully.

LET'S REVIEW

The female slave in today's reading was in the lowest class of her social structure, yet she proclaimed the way to freedom for her neighbors in Philippi. How do you think our society's standards of value cause us to give one person's voice more weight than that of another?

The slave girl's value to her masters was defined solely by the wealth she could bring them. How do you think our culture's emphasis on the importance of wealth makes it difficult to see our neighbors as beautiful image bearers of God?

Today's reading ends with Paul and Silas in prison and the fate of the slave girl unknown. Imagine if the young church in Philippi bravely continued to reflect God's good and equitable kingdom to her. What do you think her future would have looked like?

APPLICATION

Slavery was woven into the fabric of Paul's world.[2] Slaves comprised as much as 20 percent of the population in the Roman empire. These slaves had no rights. Their masters were free to use, and abuse, them however they wanted.

Ancient Roman culture was firmly rooted in the philosophy that "Might makes right." If one was strong enough to assert dominion over another, he was free to do so. When we read accounts of the brutal gladiatorial games or see images from Pompeii in which slaves remain chained together in death as they were in life, we are understandably horrified.

This brutality, however, was part of the very air Paul breathed. It must have been a small miracle for anyone in such a world to even be able to see the crushing injustice right in front of them.

We don't know if Paul was able to have compassion for the slave girl in today's reading. We are only told that he set her free from the demon that bound her because he was really "annoyed" by her proclamations.

It is important to remember that Paul's motivation was not necessarily reflective of Christ's purposes in this moment. Paul was a brilliant, God-loving, redeemed, but *flawed* product of his environment. Sadly, Scripture gives us no reason to believe that Paul set this girl free because he had compassion on her.

We must never forget, however, that if God had not willed her to be free, Paul would have been powerless to cast the demon out of her. Paul may or may not have been able to see this girl in her need, but Jesus certainly did.

This small moment in Scripture, which ended with Paul in prison for the first time, provides for us a stark contrast between the Roman world, enslaved by idolatry and the forces of evil, and the kingdom of God.

In the Roman world, worth was defined by power and position. Jesus, however, set a different standard:

> You know that the rulers of the Gentiles lord it over them, and those who are great exercise authority over them. Yet it shall not be so among you; but whoever desires to become great among you, let him be your servant. And whoever desires to be first among you, let him be your slave— just as the Son of Man did not come to be served, but to serve, and to give His life a ransom for many. (Matthew 20:25–28 NKJV)

When the kingdom of God breaks through into our lives, it will inevitably challenge our perceptions both of ourselves and of others. The wise follower of Christ will humbly seek God in prayer, asking Him to give them eyes to see as He sees and a heart that loves as He loves.

[2]https://www.britishmuseum.org/exhibitions/nero-man-behind-myth/slavery-ancient-rome

PROMPT

Take time to pray about this. Write a prayer to God and ask Him to show you where you have adopted a fallen world's standard of worth over His own and ask Him to give you a heart like His.

DIG DEEPER

Isaiah 42:1–8
Isaiah 61:1–3
Psalm 102:16–20

DAY 16

Prison Bars Open

Paul and Silas, wounded and bleeding, followed the prison guard down the stone steps and into the dungeon. Prisoners with heavy chains around their ankles filled the space. Some lay on the filthy stone floor. Others sat with their backs against the walls. A few lifted eyes filled with misery to observe the newcomers, but Paul and Silas were only there for a moment. The guard had specific instructions to keep the two new men in his charge under the tightest security he could provide, and that meant they were headed below.

A foul stench rose from a hole cut into the stone floor. It was the entrance to the innermost part of the prison, where the most dangerous criminals were kept as they awaited their fate. The guard lowered a ladder, and the two men descended into the dark, the guard behind them with a torch.

He led them to their cell, chained them, and then left them to suffer, the heavy gate clanging shut behind him. As the torch receded down the passageway, the room grew steadily dimmer until, at last, Paul and Silas were plunged into absolute darkness.

Minutes slipped into hours as all sense of time was lost amid the groans of the other prisoners, the skittering of vermin, and the overwhelming agony of their own wounds.

So Paul and Silas turned their hearts to the comfort and hope of God. Soon, the sound of their voices lifted in prayer, and praise echoed off the stone walls and down the dark corridors, offering hope and comfort to the suffering men and women.

At midnight, the earth began to shake. The walls groaned as the floor rolled beneath them. The prisoners' chains rattled and fell off as the heavy iron gates to their cells swung open with a crash. The prisoners cried out in terror.

After what seemed like an eternity, the tremors stilled and all grew quiet.

From somewhere in the distance came the guard's cry and the sound of his sword pulling out of its sheath as he realized the prisoners were free. There was no doubt in anyone's mind as to his intention. Death was preferable to the torture he would endure for allowing the prisoners to escape.

Paul shouted into the darkness for him to stop, assuring him that everyone was still there. The guard called for a torch and rushed to Paul and Silas, fell before them trembling, and asked what he could do to be saved.

His hope, desperate as it was, was simply for a way out of the predicament he was in. All Romans knew that the gods sent earthquakes when they were angry. The guard needed a way to appease them, a way out, before things got worse. Paul, however, knew the salvation he needed was far greater. He needed Jesus the Messiah.

The guard heard the good news of the Gospel and believed. He led Paul and Silas out of the dungeon, up into the fresh air, and into his own home. After he washed and dressed their wounds, Paul baptized him and his whole household. Salvation had come, and it was a far greater salvation than the prison guard had ever dreamed of.

His chains were gone.

SCRIPTURE READING

Read the dramatic account of Paul and Silas's first trip to prison and their shocking deliverance below.

Acts 16:23–34 NRSV

After they had given them a severe flogging, they threw them into prison and ordered the jailer to keep them securely. Following these instructions, he put them in the innermost cell and fastened their feet in the stocks. About midnight Paul and Silas were praying and singing hymns to God, and the prisoners were listening to them. Suddenly there was an earthquake, so violent that the foundations of the prison were shaken; and immediately all the doors were opened and everyone's chains were unfastened. When the jailer woke up and saw the prison doors wide open, he drew his sword and was about to kill himself, since he supposed that the prisoners had escaped. But Paul shouted in a loud voice, "Do not harm yourself, for we are all here." The jailer called for lights, and rushing in, he fell down trembling before Paul and Silas. Then he brought them outside and said, "Sirs, what must I do to be saved?" They answered, "Believe on the Lord Jesus, and you will be saved, you and your household." They spoke the word of the Lord to him and to all who were in his house. At the same hour of the night he took them and washed their wounds; then he and his entire family were baptized without delay. He brought them up into the house and set food before them; and he and his entire household rejoiced that he had become a believer in God.

LET'S REVIEW

Roman prisons were horrible dungeons where prisoners awaited their final judgment. Surprisingly, Paul and Silas prayed and sang hymns despite their suffering.

Do you respond with worship when you experience suffering? Why or why not?

Whenever the earth began to roll, which happened frequently in this region, the Romans believed it was because the gods were angry. When the guard asked Paul and Silas what he needed to do to be saved, he wasn't referring to spiritual salvation. He wanted to know how to save his skin! But Paul offered him a more powerful form of rescue, one that was eternal.

Why do you think we sometimes become fixated on "salvation" from a physical situation to the point that we lose sight of what God wants to do in our hearts?

In his writings, Paul repeatedly asserts that the life-giving, restoring power of the Gospel would spread through the suffering of Jesus' followers. How do you see this at work in today's reading?

APPLICATION

Roman prisons were designed to break their inhabitants through their horrible conditions. They were filthy, vermin infested, and dark. In a very real sense, time spent in a Roman prison was torture that stripped those confined there of every shred of dignity.

In today's remarkable reading, we see the kingdom of God on full display. The Roman world's values were shaped by their worship of the gods, idols through which the Evil One degraded those who worshiped them, bound them, and robbed them of their humanity.

As Paul and Silas prayed and sang hymns in the innermost room of that horrific prison, their backs wounded and bleeding, it must have seemed as if the dark forces of evil had won. Instead, God was at work to rescue the guard and his entire family from the bondage under which they had lived their whole lives.

The guard left Paul and Silas in the dungeon to suffer, and possibly even die, but when they realized he was about to take his own life, they intervened. He had bound them with chains and locked them behind gates of iron, but they offered him freedom from the bondage of idolatry under which he had lived his whole life.

When he bowed trembling before them, terrified, asking for "salvation," a way out of the mess he was in, they offered him and his entire family salvation for their souls.

The kingdom of God relentlessly restores the broken, lifts the oppressed, and sets the captive free.

Are you asking for a big enough salvation today? God is ready to break your chains.

restore the broken

PROMPT

Write a prayer to God asking Him to show you a place in your life where you have asked for a salvation that is much too small. Then write His answer.

DIG DEEPER

Psalm 68:5–7
Psalm 79:10–11
Psalm 31:1–2

DAY 17

Where God Lives

Paul was in trouble again.

This time, he was alone and far from home in the great city of Athens. He was separated from his traveling companions after fleeing another angry mob, enraged by his teaching, in the city of Berea.

After arriving in Athens, it didn't take him long to stir up enough conflict to find his life hanging in the balance once again. This time, it was especially serious. He had been brought before the highest court in Athens, the Areopagus, on the charge of introducing foreign deities. It was the same charge for which the philosopher, Socrates, had been condemned to death by drinking a potion of hemlock in Athens four hundred years before.

When Paul arrived in Athens, he followed his pattern of sharing the news of Jesus in the synagogue first, and then took his debate to the philosophers in the marketplace.

One might expect a stranger, alone in a huge city, to proceed cautiously after having so recently barely escaped with his life, but Paul knew nothing about holding back. He took on the philosophers of Athens with gusto.

When they couldn't out-reason him, they seized him and took him to the Areopagus for judgment.

With the magnificent temple of Athena, the Parthenon, looming in the background, the distinguished members of the court leveled steely gazes at the Jewish man before them. He wasn't very impressive. His clothing was worn from endless travel, his skin streaked with scars from beatings and stoning.

His eyes, however, shone with fierce intelligence. When they invited him to make his defense, they had no idea what awaited them. This man, whose mind was whip sharp, was the product of two worlds—one deeply Jewish, the other Roman. He had both mastered the Scriptures and developed the rhetorical skills of a philosopher while growing up in Tarsus.

Carefully, masterfully, Paul built his argument, not only defending himself, but also attacking the very foundation upon which they built their entire society—their worship of the gods. He used their own philosophies against them, turning them inside out to reveal their flaws.

With a dismissive glance in the direction of the Parthenon, home to a huge statue of Athena, goddess of wisdom and war, Paul announced that the one true God who created heaven and earth had no need for mere mortals to build Him a house. As a matter of fact, He didn't need anything from them at all.

Paul wrapped things up by telling them that God had been gracious to them in their idolatry but that time was running out. The resurrected Christ was ready to hold them accountable, and they had better repent.

Somehow, miraculously, Paul escaped his own cup of hemlock. Instead, the council laughed the strange little man off the stage and sent him on his way. His arguments, however, lingered, leaving the philosophers and judges of Athens to ponder the columned marble edifice a few hundred yards away, home to the goddess of wisdom and war.

A goddess sculpted by human hands.

A goddess made of stone.

A goddess who never answered when they called.

SCRIPTURE READING

Read the Scripture below for the account of Paul's speech before the Areopagus.

Acts 17:16–34 NRSV

While Paul was waiting for them in Athens, he was deeply distressed to see that the city was full of idols. So he argued in the synagogue with the Jews and the devout persons, and also in the marketplace every day with those who happened to be there. Also some Epicurean and Stoic philosophers debated with him. Some said, "What does this babbler want to say?" Others said, "He seems to be a proclaimer of foreign divinities." (This was because he was telling the good news about Jesus and the resurrection.) So they took him and brought him to the Areopagus and asked him, "May we know what this new teaching is that you are presenting? It sounds rather strange to us, so we would like to know what it means." Now all the Athenians and the foreigners living there would spend their time in nothing but telling or hearing something new.

Then Paul stood in front of the Areopagus and said, "Athenians, I see how extremely religious you are in every way. For as I went through the city and looked carefully at the objects of your worship, I found among them an altar with the inscription, 'To an unknown god.' What therefore you worship as unknown, this I proclaim to you. The God who made the world and everything in it, he who is Lord of heaven and earth, does not live in shrines made by human hands, nor is He served by human hands, as though He needed anything, since He Himself gives to all mortals life and breath and all things. From one ancestor He made all nations to inhabit the whole earth, and He allotted the times of their existence and the boundaries of the places where they would live, so that they would search for God and perhaps grope for Him and find Him—though indeed He is not far from each one of us. For 'In him we live and move and have our being'; as even some of your own poets have said,

'For we too are his offspring.'

Since we are God's offspring, we ought not to think that the deity is like gold, or silver, or stone, an image formed by the art and imagination of mortals. While God has overlooked the times of human ignorance, now He commands all people everywhere to repent, because He has fixed a day on which He will have the world judged in righteousness by a man whom He has appointed, and of this He has given assurance to all by raising Him from the dead."

When they heard of the resurrection of the dead, some scoffed; but others said, "We will hear you again about this." At that point Paul left them. But some of them joined him and became believers, including Dionysius the Areopagite and a woman named Damaris, and others with them.

LET'S REVIEW

The Areopagus was the highest court in Athens. Its judges held the power of life and death over the accused who were brought to them. How do you think Paul felt as he was brought before them?

As Paul made his defense, he took the opportunity to spread the Gospel. In the second paragraph of our Scripture reading, what does Paul say about the one true God and shrines?

Paul says that God "made all nations to inhabit the whole earth, and he allotted the times of their existence and the boundaries of the places where they would live" (Acts 17:26 NRSV). What does he say God's purpose was in this?

APPLICATION

Our story today is the story of two deities—one false, one true—and the places they call home.

The Athenians invested incredible resources to build the Parthenon, temple of their patron goddess, Athena. The columned marble structure, 101 feet wide by 228 feet long, was a breathtaking feat of ancient design and engineering. In 438 BC, the same year the Parthenon was completed, Athenians placed a thirty-eight-foot ivory and gold statue of Athena inside. The silent, unmoving goddess of wisdom and war was home.

The Jews had their own idea about where God lived: the temple in Jerusalem. During His earthly ministry, however, Jesus refuted that idea. He taught that the temple was merely a symbol pointing to Himself. Through Jesus, God came to live among us. He put on human flesh and called this broken creation He loves home.

In I Corinthians 1:3–16, Paul takes the analogy a step further. He writes that we, the redeemed, are the temple of God and that Jesus is our foundation.

When the Jews began clearing the rubble of the sanctuary from the First Temple in preparation to rebuild, they discovered a stone in the center of the former holy of holies. It was the stone on which the priest would place the pan with the offering of incense, which represented the prayers of the people, once each year on the Day of Atonement. The name of the stone was *Shetiyah*, which is translated "foundation" (Bailey, 2011).

Jesus, through His sacrifice on the cross, entered the Holy of Holies, completed the work of atonement, and made way for God to come even closer. Because of Jesus, the Spirit of God now lives *within* us.

When Paul defended himself before the Areopagus, he was also fighting for the souls of the Athenians. He longed to free them from their worship of a statue of stone, made by their own hands. Athena had a beautiful home, but she would forever remain silent, unmoving, unspeaking, unable to save.

Paul offered the Athenians the living God, the One who created all things yet had humbled Himself to draw near to His fallen creatures.

We are God's temple, built upon the foundation of Jesus Christ. He hears. He speaks. He is mighty to save, and He has made His home in us.

He is mighty to save

PROMPT

What an incredible gift it is to have the Spirit of God living in us! Write a note to God expressing your gratitude for this.

DIG DEEPER

I Corinthians 6:19–20
Psalm 50:11–12
John 2:18–22

DAY 18

The Light of Jesus' Love

Oxen strained against their yokes, struggling to move heavy loads of marble, timber, bronze, and stone on the wooden platforms rolling along the grooved Diolkos, a three-and-a-half-mile, stone-paved stretch of the Isthmus of Corinth. The lowing of the animals mingled with the groans and cries of the slaves as their masters' whips fell across their backs.

Behind Paul lay the city of Athens, before him, the great city of Corinth. Several days' travel along the Lechaion Road had brought Paul to the thriving metropolis, home to three hundred thousand citizens and at least as many slaves.

Everywhere Paul looked, magnificent buildings rose from the ground, their porticoes rimmed with columns and their façades cloaked in marble. Civic centers and public baths were adorned with elaborate mosaics, and markets buzzed with activity as money from the wealthy flowed freely. In the northwest section of the city rose a semicircular theater, its fifty-five rows of seats offering ample accommodations for up to fourteen thousand spectators.

Temples to the gods were everywhere, but none more prominent than that of Aphrodite, goddess of love and fertility. Her temple sat atop the Acrocorinth, a promontory of rock to the southwest of the city so steep that it was a two-hour climb from the base to the top.

It was easy to be swept up in the excitement of Corinth. For those with means, it was a playground in which to indulge their every whim and fantasy. For Corinth's thousands of slaves, its streets were merciless and cruel.

Each evening, Paul watched as a thousand slave-prostitutes made their way into the city for their bodies to be used and abused so Aphrodite's coffers might overflow with riches. Wearily, they took their places around the beautiful Lower Fountain of Peirene, their eyes vacant and hopeless.

That these poor souls suffered in service to the "goddess of love" was bitter irony. There was no "love" for them. Corinth was rich and greedy, a place where half the population suffered so the other half might be entertained.

It was into this midnight of human suffering and degradation that Paul had come to shine the redeeming, restoring love of Jesus. He preached in the synagogues. He proclaimed Jesus in the streets.

And souls hungry for redemption believed.

This is how Timothy and Silas found Paul when they finally caught up with him. Together they nurtured the church at Corinth for eighteen months. When they moved on to Ephesus, they left behind an outpost of the kingdom of God tasked with radiating the light of Jesus in a city cloaked in the dark forces of evil.

Later, while Paul was in Ephesus, he received disturbing news about the church in Corinth. Instead of pushing back against the forces of oppression, they were bringing the dehumanizing, self-serving morality of Corinth into the church! Abandoning the command to love their neighbors as themselves, they were using their liberty in Christ as an excuse to indulge themselves at the cost of the suffering of others.

Some members gluttonously and drunkenly partook of the Lord's Supper, leaving others with empty plates and cups. Others continued to victimize the temple prostitutes, satiating their sexual appetites at the expense of slave girls who had no choice but to comply.

It was even reported that one man had begun preying on his father's wife, a crime not even the Romans would have tolerated if they had known about it. Instead of responding with horror and shame, the other members of the church were arrogantly boasting about the scandal.

As member after member turned from the love of God and neighbor to the service of self, a light that was meant to shine brightly, guiding those enslaved by evil to the resurrection freedom of Jesus, wavered and dimmed until it was in danger of being snuffed out completely.

Paul was horrified. Enraged. With pen and scroll in hand, he furiously wrote to the church in Corinth, urging them to repent and live out the love of Christ, and in doing so, set the captives free.

SCRIPTURE READING

When we cease to obey God's command to love our neighbors as ourselves, we inevitably harm them. Read Paul's beautiful tribute to the power of love below.

I Corinthians 13:1–13 NRSV

If I speak in the tongues of mortals and of angels, but do not have love, I am a noisy gong or a clanging cymbal. And if I have prophetic powers, and understand all mysteries and all knowledge, and if I have all faith, so as to remove mountains, but do not have love, I am nothing. If I give away all my possessions, and if I hand over my body so that I may boast, but do not have love, I gain nothing.

Love is patient; love is kind; love is not envious or boastful or arrogant or rude. It does not insist on its own way; it is not irritable or resentful; it does not rejoice in wrongdoing, but rejoices in the truth. It bears all things, believes all things, hopes all things, endures all things.

Love never ends. But as for prophecies, they will come to an end; as for tongues, they will cease; as for knowledge, it will come to an end. For we know only in part, and we prophesy only in part; but when the complete comes, the partial will come to an end. When I was a child, I spoke like a child, I thought like a child, I reasoned like a child; when I became an adult, I put an end to childish ways. For now we see in a mirror, dimly, but then we will see face to face. Now I know only in part; then I will know fully, even as I have been fully known. And now faith, hope, and love abide, these three; and the greatest of these is love.

LET'S REVIEW

Our Scripture reading says that love doesn't "rejoice in wrongdoing." How is this in stark contrast with the culture of Corinth, particularly in their worship of Aphrodite?

The skilled craftsmen of Corinth often made mirrors out of brass and would etch an image of their customer's god of choice on the surface. This way, when they looked at their reflection in the mirror, they saw themselves with the gods. In our Scripture reading today, Paul references this in a metaphor. What does he say will be the difference in how we "see" Jesus now and how we will see Him upon his return?

In the final verse of this beautiful passage, Paul says that three gifts will last forever: faith, hope, and love. Which of these does he say is the greatest? Why do you think that is?

APPLICATION

Throughout history, human beings have inflicted unspeakable suffering on each other. A worldview that values elevation and indulgence of self allows one to dismiss the humanity of others and use them however one sees fit.

This worship of self is perhaps the most basic instinct of the fallen flesh, and in the Roman world, it was considered a right rather than an injustice. If a man was powerful enough or wealthy enough to use a fellow human being for his own gain—or even entertainment—he was expected to do so.

When Jesus came, He showed us a radically different way of living. During His ministry, He challenged His followers to give away their resources, warning them that it was difficult for a rich man to enter the kingdom of heaven. He fed the hungry, touched lepers, and furiously cleared the temple courts when merchants were taking advantage of worshipers.

In the ultimate sacrifice, He gave His very life to free us, and all of creation, from the curse of sin.

Removed from the debauchery of Corinth, we pass judgment on their sin, but how often do we allow our fallen world's values to creep into our lives and crowd out the love of Christ? How often do we forget that the people our society considers the least valuable are precious image bearers of God whom we are called to love as ourselves?

Thankfully, God has not left us without a witness and guide. He has given us His Holy Spirit to show us how to live a life pleasing to Him and empower us to do so. In this way, we will shine the light of God's love into a world of darkness, restoring the broken, healing the wounded, and setting the captives free.

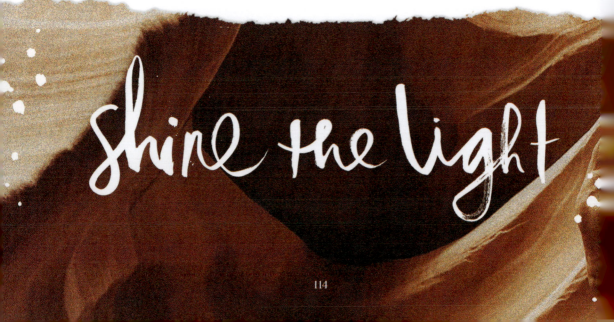
shine the light

PROMPT

Describe a time in your life when you traded the values of a fallen world for those of the kingdom of heaven. What was the outcome? How did it affect those around you? Then write a prayer to Jesus, thanking Him for setting you free from any shame or guilt, and for restoring all that is broken.

DIG DEEPER

I Thessalonians 5:1–10
I Corinthians 6:15–20
Acts 18:1–18

DAY 19

Success, Failure, and the Power of God

A roar. Screams. The sounds of pottery crashing to the floor and bodies slamming against the walls.

At last, the door bangs open, and seven men run out into the street, eyes wide with terror. They are bloody, bruised, and completely naked.

Welcome to Ephesus.

Paul is at the top of his game. He is working as a tentmaker while teaching huge crowds. Even more remarkably, he has been filled with a special manifestation of the Holy Spirit. Everywhere he goes, he heals the sick and frees the demon-possessed. The power of God flows through him so strongly that even handkerchiefs that touch his skin have the power to heal. The crowds can't quit talking about it.

He is an absolute sensation. It is this—his fame and popularity—that lead to the moment when seven sons of the high priest Sceva had an unfortunate encounter with a demon-possessed man.

All the sons of Sceva wanted was a little of the glory, and perhaps to have their palms lined along the way. So they came up with the perfect scheme. They would hitch a ride on the back of this power flowing through Paul. They began using his name, and the name of Jesus, in an attempt to cast out demons.

Until the day when they crossed the wrong demon.

The sons of Sceva stood before the possessed man and ordered the demon to leave him in the name of Jesus and Paul. The demon in turn told them that he knew who Jesus and Paul were, but that he had no idea who they were. Then he gave them a thorough trashing and sent them running into the street.

If the citizens of Ephesus were excited about Paul's ministry before, they are completely in awe now. More men and women come to believe in Jesus the Messiah. Those who had once practiced the dark arts turn from their ways and publicly burn their expensive spell books. The power of the Gospel has the forces of evil on the run.

Unfortunately for Paul, it is an insult those forces won't take lightly. They aren't finished with him yet—a painful truth he would discover all too soon.

SCRIPTURE READING

Read the Scripture below for the account of this exciting season of Paul's ministry.

Acts 19:11–20 NRSV

God did extraordinary miracles through Paul, so that when the handkerchiefs or aprons that had touched his skin were brought to the sick, their diseases left them, and the evil spirits came out of them. Then some itinerant Jewish exorcists tried to use the name of the Lord Jesus over those who had evil spirits, saying, "I adjure you by the Jesus whom Paul proclaims." Seven sons of a Jewish high priest named Sceva were doing this. But the evil spirit said to them in reply, "Jesus I know, and Paul I know; but who are you?" Then the man with the evil spirit leaped on them, mastered them all, and so overpowered them that they fled out of the house naked and wounded. When this became known to all residents of Ephesus, both Jews and Greeks, everyone was awestruck; and the name of the Lord Jesus was praised. Also many of those who became believers confessed and disclosed their practices. A number of those who practiced magic collected their books and burned them publicly; when the value of these books was calculated, it was found to come to fifty thousand silver coins. So the word of the Lord grew mightily and prevailed.

What happened when the cloths that had touched Paul's skin were brought to the sick and possessed?

In whose names were the seven sons of Sceva attempting to exorcise demons? What did the evil spirit say to them when they attempted to cast it out?

Although Paul certainly became well known because of these events, what was the primary result of these miracles?

APPLICATION

Sometimes we are blessed with a season when everything seems to go right. During those times, it is tempting to pat ourselves on the back for making the right choices or working hard. Perhaps we even begin to believe that we are special in some way and deserve our success.

The hard truth is that our faithfulness does not always lead to success. There are those who love and serve God with sincerity and fidelity with little earthly reward for their efforts. This doesn't mean the power of God was absent from their lives. One of the great mysteries of faith is that God's power is often at work in the hidden places, in the shadowy realms of service that God alone sees.

Perhaps the greatest, most Spirit-empowered work of our lives is demonstrated not publicly but in the secret places of our minds and hearts—the moments when we choose to bless those who curse us, forgive those who betray us, and love those who most deeply wound us. These are acts of service that we are utterly incapable of performing apart from the mighty power of God.

In today's Scripture reading, the sons of Sceva tried to harness the power of God for their own benefit, and it backfired on them, granting them public humiliation rather than praise. Paul, however, kept his focus on his service rather than his reputation, and God received the glory.

The goal of our service to God is not success or failure, but rather faithfully following where God leads. This is how we lay up treasures in heaven, "where neither moth nor rust consumes and where thieves do not break in and steal" (Matthew 6:20 NRSV).

The power and the glory is God's alone.

the power and the glory is god's alone

PROMPT

When in your life have you experienced success and failure? Journal about how these moments impacted your faith.

DIG DEEPER

Psalm 66:1–4
Ephesians 6:12
II Corinthians 2:14

DAY 20

The Riot in Ephesus

"Great is Artemis of the Ephesians! Great is Artemis of the Ephesians!"

The chant echoed through the city, past archways, and down columned streets. It floated out over the manmade harbor and up to the Temple of Artemis itself. It rang throughout palatial mansions, and finally, through the humble walls of the house where Paul and his friends were staying.

This was all his fault, and he desperately wanted to fix it. As soon as he realized what was happening, he made for the door, ready to march onto the stage of the theater where the crowd had gathered to make his case. His friends wouldn't allow it. It was far too dangerous. Who knew what might happen to Paul at the hands of thousands of furious Ephesians?

The chant began with a group of silversmiths who were drawn together by a craftsman named Demetrius after he realized that Paul's preaching against gods "made by human hands" was seriously hurting business. He and his fellow artisans made a lot of money from the silver statues of the goddess Artemis. Practically every home in Ephesus had a shrine with at least one displayed to which they would pray and offer gifts in the hope that the goddess of fertility would bless their businesses and homes.

Demetrius had watched the silver statues sitting idle on the shelves of his shop long enough. He had wearied of the slackening weight of his moneybag. It was time to act. So he called together the other silversmiths and made his case that not only was Paul hurting their previously good income, he was also defaming the glorious Temple of Artemis, and the goddess as well, in the process.

The Temple of Artemis was the pride of Ephesus and is considered one of the seven wonders of the ancient world. The massive marble structure, four times the size of the Parthenon, was rimmed with 120 columns more than 60 feet tall and 6 feet thick. Thirty-six of them were overlaid with gold. Inside the temple, a eunuch high priest and virgin priestesses attended to a huge statue of the fertility goddess, which was believed to have been gifted to Ephesus by Zeus himself. The temple, however, was more than the epicenter of Ephesian religious life; it was also a bank.

When Demetrius explained to the other silversmiths why their businesses had taken a nosedive, they were infuriated. They rushed out into the street chanting in rage. Soon, a large crowd joined in, and the mob rushed into the three-story, twenty-four-thousand-seat theater. There, the acoustics amplified their voices until the whole city shook with the racket.

Paul and his friends paced and prayed. Two of their group, Gaius and Aristarchus, had been seized by the angry mob. There was little doubt that their lives were in grave danger.

Finally, after what seemed like an eternity, the men heard the chant fall silent. One of the city magistrates had managed to diffuse the situation and send everyone back to their businesses and homes.

The bitter resentment held by those whose businesses had been hurt by Paul's teaching, however, would linger. After all, Artemis might have been beloved by the Ephesians, but only for what they hoped she could provide—bountiful crops, burgeoning businesses, and healthy bank accounts.

It was all about the money—money in the marketplace and money in the temple bank. Paul had crossed a line, one that Demetrius and his friends were unlikely to forgive anytime soon.

SCRIPTURE READING

Read the Scripture below for a firsthand account of the riot in Ephesus.

Acts 19:23–41 NIV

About that time there arose a great disturbance about the Way. A silversmith named Demetrius, who made silver shrines of Artemis, brought in a lot of business for the craftsmen there. He called them together, along with the workers in related trades, and said: "You know, my friends, that we receive a good income from this business. And you see and hear how this fellow Paul has convinced and led astray large numbers of people here in Ephesus and in practically the whole province of Asia. He says that gods made by human hands are no gods at all. There is danger not only that our trade will lose its good name, but also that the temple of the great goddess Artemis will be discredited; and the goddess herself, who is worshiped throughout the province of Asia and the world, will be robbed of her divine majesty."

When they heard this, they were furious and began shouting: "Great is Artemis of the Ephesians!" Soon the whole city was in an uproar. The people seized Gaius and Aristarchus, Paul's traveling companions from Macedonia, and all of them rushed into the theater together. Paul wanted to appear before the crowd, but the disciples would not let him. Even some of the officials of the province, friends of Paul, sent him a message begging him not to venture into the theater.

The assembly was in confusion: Some were shouting one thing, some another. Most of the people did not even know why they were there. The Jews in the crowd pushed Alexander to the front, and they shouted instructions to him. He motioned for silence in order to make a defense before the people. But when they realized he was a Jew, they all shouted in unison for about two hours: "Great is Artemis of the Ephesians!"

The city clerk quieted the crowd and said: "Fellow Ephesians, doesn't all the world know that the city of Ephesus is the guardian of the temple of the great Artemis and of her image, which fell from heaven? Therefore, since these facts are undeniable, you ought to calm down and not do anything rash. You have brought these men here, though they have neither robbed temples nor blasphemed our goddess. If, then, Demetrius and his fellow craftsmen have a grievance against anybody, the courts are open and there are proconsuls. They can press charges. If there is anything further you want to bring up, it must be settled in a legal assembly. As it is, we are in danger of being charged with rioting because of what happened today. In that case we would not be able to account for this commotion, since there is no reason for it." After he had said this, he dismissed the assembly.

Demetrius warned his fellow craftsmen that Paul was a threat. What two dangers did he say Paul's teaching presented?

Our Scripture says that the mob chanted for two hours. What were they chanting?

When the city clerk calmed the crowd, he gave them instructions on the proper way to handle their grievances. What did he say they should do instead of rioting?

APPLICATION

In Paul's first letter to Timothy, he warned the young man that "the love of money is a root of all kinds of evil" (I Timothy 6:10 NRSV). In today's Scripture reading, the destructive power of money is on full display. When Paul's teachings began to free the Ephesians from their slavery to idolatry, he inadvertently hurt the bank accounts of some local silversmiths who had been profiting from their neighbors' worship of Artemis. A mob was whipped into a fury, and all of a sudden, Paul and his friends were in danger.

Perhaps the root of the love of money is the fear of scarcity, a fear that goes all the way back to the Garden of Eden. Adam and Eve had everything they could possibly want or need in paradise, and yet, somehow, a few deceptive words from Satan lodged a seed of doubt in their hearts.

What if God was holding out on them?

What if that one tree He said to leave alone was the secret to everything?

What if paradise wasn't enough?

The fear of scarcity has been passed down from Adam and Eve through countless generations. As it has made its way through the annals of history, it has left a wake of destruction in its path—wars and invasions, famine and oppression, friends and families torn apart.

Jesus once warned His disciples that they couldn't serve both God and money. If Paul's writings have taught us anything, it is that the worship of anything other than God is idolatry, and idolatry is slavery.

God wants us to be free. He wants us to bring our needs to Him with the simple trust of a small child. Our God is a God of abundance in whose hands are all the resources in the world.

Let go of the love of money and the slavery it brings. Take your needs to your abundant God and leave them in His faithful hands. In Him, you have all you need.

in god we have all we need

PROMPT

Are you worried about provision today? Journal all your concerns below and then write a prayer, leaving them in His faithful hands.

DIG DEEPER

I Timothy 6:6–10
Matthew 6:19–24
II Timothy 3:1–5

DAY 21

A God Who Sets the Captives Free

The darkness. The filth. The cries of men condemned to die.

Paul was in prison again, this time in Ephesus.

He kept himself as busy as he could. He wrote letters. Meditated on Scripture and prayed. Still, as the days and weeks bled one into another, his body and soul grew weary.

Sometimes he had visitors, friends who came to bring him food and minister to his needs. He was always grateful for their company and provisions. Then, one day, a new visitor arrived. It was a young man, a stranger so frightened and alone that he had come to Paul, a prisoner, for help.

His name was Onesimus, and he was a runaway slave.

Paul listened to his story and discovered that this slave belonged to a friend of his, Philemon. Philemon was a fellow believer living 150 miles away in Colossae who had come to faith in Jesus while visiting Ephesus.

Paul shared the Gospel with Onesimus, and the runaway slave found true freedom in Christ. Then the young man devoted himself to caring for Paul in prison. He was faithful and a true encouragement. Over time, Paul began to consider him a son.

But the apostle knew he had to address the situation between Onesimus and Philemon. Ultimately, he decided that the best course of action was far from easy. He would send the runaway slave back to his master in the hope that the same God who reconciled both men to Himself through the sacrifice of Jesus would, in turn, reconcile them to each other.

If the reconciliation power of Jesus was going to do its good work between Onesimus and Philemon, all three men would need to follow Christ's example of sacrifice on the cross.

Onesimus would take up his cross by returning to his master in obedience to Paul.

Philemon would need to take up his cross by forgiving—and freeing—his slave so that he might become a brother instead.

Paul would take up his cross by asking his friend to charge him with any debt Onesimus owed him.

It was a costly sacrifice of love all the way around. It was the way of the cross.

SCRIPTURE READING

Read Paul's plea to Philemon for Onesimus below.

Philemon 8–21 NRSV

For this reason, though I am bold enough in Christ to command you to do your duty, yet I would rather appeal to you on the basis of love—and I, Paul, do this as an old man, and now also as a prisoner of Christ Jesus. I am appealing to you for my child, Onesimus, whose father I have become during my imprisonment. Formerly he was useless to you, but now he is indeed useful both to you and to me. I am sending him, that is, my own heart, back to you. I wanted to keep him with me, so that he might be of service to me in your place during my imprisonment for the gospel; but I preferred to do nothing without your consent, in order that your good deed might be voluntary and not something forced. Perhaps this is the reason he was separated from you for a while, so that you might have him back forever, no longer as a slave but more than a slave, a beloved brother—especially to me but how much more to you, both in the flesh and in the Lord.

So if you consider me your partner, welcome him as you would welcome me. If he has wronged you in any way, or owes you anything, charge that to my account. I, Paul, am writing this with my own hand: I will repay it. I say nothing about your owing me even your own self. Yes, brother, let me have this benefit from you in the Lord! Refresh my heart in Christ. Confident of your obedience, I am writing to you, knowing that you will do even more than I say.

LET'S REVIEW

Paul says he could command Philemon to do the right thing about Onesimus. On what basis does he appeal to his friend instead?

Onesimus was a slave, and Philemon was his master. Paul, however, dreams of a better relationship between the two men. What does Paul say he hopes the slave will become to his master?

How do you think Onesimus felt as he was returning to the master from whom he had run away?

APPLICATION

The cross is the thread that runs throughout Paul's letter to Philemon.

As a runaway slave, Onesimus was in danger of crucifixion. Then his life was changed forever through the sacrifice of a Savior who *chose* to die a slave's death on the cross.

Paul challenged both Onesimus and Philemon to take up their cross by asking each of them to die to themselves so that they might be reconciled to each other. Philemon was asked to give up the right to his slave, to receive him as a brother instead (a radical concept in the ancient world). Onesimus was asked to return to his master and risk punishment or even death in the hope that Philemon would do the right thing by him.

Paul demonstrated for both men what it looked like to take up his cross when he told Philemon to charge him with any wrongs Onesimus had committed and to receive the runaway slave as he would the apostle.

Through the cross we are reconciled to God. In taking up our own crosses, God makes a way for us to be reconciled to each other. It is a beautiful mystery that is often painful to live out. Dying to self is never easy, but a glorious resurrection awaits us on the other side.

god makes a way

PROMPT

What future do you hope Onesimus found on the other side of returning to his master? Is there someone with whom you need to reconcile today? Will Paul's example influence your life today? Why or why not?

DIG DEEPER

I Peter 4:8
Proverbs 10:12
Luke 9:23

DAY 22

The Redemption of Suffering

Lamplight flickered along the wall as Paul descended the steps of the *mikveh*, a ritual bath for purification. He allowed the water to cover him completely before climbing the second set of steps, emerging back into the bright Middle Eastern sun.

He had completed the seven-day process of ritual purification as the leaders of the Jerusalem church had asked. But would it be enough to appease the zealous Jews who were enraged by his ministry to the Gentiles?

Paul looked up at the towering temple complex above him. He knew its courts and porticoes as well as his own home. He had studied there under Gamaliel and offered sacrifices at Passover. He had worshiped there, and he had prayed there.

He climbed the steps to the temple gate. A moment later, he was inside.

It didn't take long for some zealous Jews from Ephesus to recognize him. In a blink, they seized him and began to shout their accusations to the crowd of worshipers. They told the crowd that not only was Paul teaching people to disobey the law, but he had also defiled the temple by bringing one of his Gentile friends into the inner courts. It wasn't true.

But a mob isn't concerned with the truth.

The Jews were infuriated. They dragged Paul into the street, slamming the temple doors behind him. Fists rained down on him until he fell beneath the blows. As he lay helpless on the ground, the mob on top of him, death seemed very near.

These were his own people. He had traveled hundreds of miles by foot to take the good news of the Messiah to their synagogues all over the Roman world. He had agonized over them and prayed endlessly that they would come to trust in Jesus.

Would his fellow Jews ever accept that their Messiah had come?

Abruptly, the beating stopped. When the mob pulled back from where Paul lay bleeding on the ground, he saw the stern face of a Roman commander standing over him. Behind the commander stood two centurions with their soldiers, their faces grim and their knuckles white around the hilts of their swords. The commander's strong hands reached down and pulled Paul to his feet before binding him with chains. He had been saved from the fury of the Jewish mob only to be arrested by the Romans.

After the commander attempted and failed to get to the root of the disturbance by questioning the crowd, he marched Paul toward the barracks, soldiers flanking him in protection.

With each step toward the Roman stronghold, the mob grew more violent, screaming for blood and pushing against the soldiers. When Paul reached the steps, they became so enraged that the soldiers were forced to lift him above their heads and carry him.

Once he was at the top of the steps, with the barracks doors in front of him, Paul turned to the commander and spoke to him in Greek. The man's eyes widened in surprise to hear the brutalized Jewish man speaking his language.

It was the opening Paul needed. He begged for permission to address the crowd, and it was granted.

Paul turned to face the mob and raised a trembling hand in a request for silence. When the crowd quieted enough for him to address them, he did so in *their* language, Aramaic.

He had one more chance.

One more chance to lead his people into the light. One more chance to point them to the truth of the Messiah. Maybe this time, they would hear him. Maybe this time, they would believe.

With burly Roman soldiers standing behind him, ready to torture him if necessary to get to the truth, and the mob that had just attempted to beat him to death standing in front of him, Paul risked everything for one more chance.

If his suffering brought his beloved people to faith in Jesus, it was worth it all.

SCRIPTURE READING

Read the Scripture below for the account of Paul's suffering at the hands of his own people.

Acts 21:17–31 NRSV

When we arrived in Jerusalem, the brothers welcomed us warmly. The next day Paul went with us to visit James; and all the elders were present. After greeting them, he related one by one the things that God had done among the Gentiles through his ministry. When they heard it, they praised God. Then they said to him, "You see, brother, how many thousands of believers there are among the Jews, and they are all zealous for the law. They have been told about you that you teach all the Jews living among the Gentiles to forsake Moses, and that you tell them not to circumcise their children or observe the customs. What then is to be done? They will certainly hear that you have come. So do what we tell you. We have four men who are under a vow. Join these men, go through the rite of purification with them, and pay for the shaving of their heads. Thus all will know that there is nothing in what they have been told about you, but that you yourself observe and guard the law. But as for the Gentiles who have become believers, we have sent a letter with our judgment that they should abstain from what has been sacrificed to idols and from blood and from what is strangled and from fornication." Then Paul took the men, and the next day, having purified himself, he entered the temple with them, making public the completion of the days of purification when the sacrifice would be made for each of them.

When the seven days were almost completed, the Jews from Asia, who had seen him in the temple, stirred up the whole crowd. They seized him, shouting, "Fellow Israelites, help! This is the man who is teaching everyone everywhere against our people, our law, and this place; more than that, he has actually brought Greeks into the temple and has defiled this holy place." For they had previously seen Trophimus the Ephesian with him in the city, and they supposed that Paul had brought him into the temple. Then all the city was aroused, and the people rushed together. They seized Paul and dragged him out of the temple, and immediately the doors were shut. While they were trying to kill him, word came to the tribune of the cohort that all Jerusalem was in an uproar.

LET'S REVIEW

What steps did the church leaders in Jerusalem suggest Paul take to try to smooth things over with the Jews? How was this supposed to help?

When the Jews from Asia saw Paul in the temple, what did they accuse him of?

How do you think Paul felt to be attacked so viciously by his own people?

APPLICATION

Paul remained a faithful Jew throughout his lifetime. For him, devotion to Jesus wasn't a new religion, it was the fulfillment of all God's promises to the Jews.

Paul loved his people, and he knew exactly where they were coming from when they rejected his message. He, too, had been zealous, sincere, and *completely blind* to the Messiah until Jesus revealed Himself on the road to Damascus. He wanted his fellow Jews to know the joyous truth that God had fulfilled His promises to them—the Messiah had come.

Our Scripture reading today finds Paul enduring horrible suffering at the hands of the people he loved. They accuse him falsely, drag him out of the temple courts, and are beating him to death when Roman soldiers step in and stop the mayhem.

Paul had every reason to be bitter. Everyone would have understood if he decided his fellow Jews were a lost cause and walked away from them forever. As a Roman citizen, he even had the power to point out his assailants to the guards and turn the tables of suffering back on them.

But he didn't. He never stopped loving them, never stopped risking his life to share with them the good news of the Messiah.

We all suffer unjustly at some point in our lives. As children of God, we, like Paul, have a unique opportunity in that moment to do the work of the kingdom of God.

In his beautiful book *Sacred Fire*, Ronald Rolheiser asserts that this is what Mary was doing as she stood silently at the foot of her Son's cross: "She is doing all that can be done when one is standing under the weight of the cross, she is holding and carrying the tension, standing in strength, refusing to give back in kind, and resisting in a deep way."

The world considers this kind of response weak, but it is far from that. The choice to take the suffering inflicted upon us by others and return love and forgiveness instead of vengeance is an act of incredible strength. It means praying through the pain until we can come to the place of seeing the one who wounded us with eyes of mercy, because we recognize that they are acting out of the poverty of their own souls.

This doesn't mean we live without boundaries. God loves us and expects us to steward our lives well. On the contrary, this type of kingdom work is done by those who know their infinite worth in Jesus. They know that the riches of all eternity are theirs and that nothing can separate them from the love of Christ. They are certain that God is more than capable of bringing them justice, and they trust Him to do so.

Empowered by the Holy Spirit, we can pray with Jesus, "Father, forgive them, for they don't know what they are doing" (Luke 23:34 NLT). Then, miraculously, there is a little less darkness in the world.

This is how our God redeems our suffering, and there is nothing more beautiful.

Is there someone you need to forgive today? Is there someone you'd go into the fire to save? How does Paul's bravery impact the way you will love people this week?

DIG DEEPER

Luke 6:27–36
Luke 22:33–38
Colossians 3:12–14

DAY 23

In the Hands of the Romans

It almost worked.

Somehow, the angry crowd had calmed down enough to hear what Paul had to say. He began by telling them his story, one like their own—his devout Jewish upbringing, his study under Gamaliel, and his zealous persecution of the followers of Christ. They even listened as he recounted meeting Jesus on the road to Damascus.

It was going so well until he mentioned his ministry to the Gentiles. Then, like a flame to tinder, the crowd exploded in rage. They were so infuriated that they ripped the cloaks from their own backs and began to throw dirt into the air as they chanted, demanding his death.

The commander of the Roman guard had seen enough. He ordered Paul brought into the barracks.

Now, already trembling with pain from the vicious beating he had just endured, Paul watched as a soldier wrapped leather thongs around his wrists, tethering him to the post before him. Another soldier stood behind him, waiting for the signal to begin the brutal flogging, because the Romans believed that the only way to get the truth from a criminal was to torture it out of him.

It was time for Paul to play his last card: his Roman citizenship.

When the soldiers learned they had almost flogged a Roman citizen without due process, they were terrified. Quickly, Paul was unbound, and after a night spent in the barracks, the commander resorted to plan B: He would bring Paul before the chief priests and Jewish council to try to resolve the matter.

Once again, violence and chaos ensued, forcing the commander to send soldiers into the fray to rescue Paul and take him back into the fortress.

That night, as Paul slept, Jesus appeared to him with encouragement and direction. His time in Jerusalem was over, and his path was finally leading to Rome, where he would proclaim the news of King Jesus at the epicenter of the Roman world.

The morning light, however, brought news of a new threat. Forty Jews had sworn to neither eat nor drink until Paul was dead. When the commander heard of the plot, he made plans to get Paul out of Jerusalem.

When night fell, Paul was brought from the barracks to find 470 soldiers—two centurions with their men, two hundred spearmen, and seventy horsemen—all waiting to escort him to Caesarea Maritima, his first stop on the way to Rome.

They rode through the night, hooves pounding beneath Paul and all around him, his aching body desperate for rest. He was surrounded by the most brutal soldiers in the world, men who knew nothing of the one true God, and yet somehow, God was using them not only to protect him, but also to speed him along to the next phase of his ministry.

The next day, Paul looked up to see the sun glinting off the Mediterranean Sea. Soon, he passed the arches of a huge aqueduct, which brought water from miles away to a beautiful city nestled up against the coast. He had arrived in Caesarea Maritima.

Paul had been rescued and protected by Roman soldiers who would now leave him in the care of a Roman governor. When the time was right, God would make the pagan empire His instrument once again to take Paul—and the good news of the Gospel—into the very heart of the empire.

Paul was safe in the hands of Rome.

SCRIPTURE READING

Read the excerpts below for an account of how God used the Romans to both protect Paul and further his mission.

Acts 22:22–30; 23:10–11, 23–24 NRSV

Paul Rescued from the Council by the Romans
Up to this point they listened to him, but then they shouted, "Away with such a fellow from the earth! For he should not be allowed to live." And while they were shouting, throwing off their cloaks, and tossing dust into the air, the tribune directed that he was to be brought into the barracks, and ordered him to be examined by flogging, to find out the reason for this outcry against him. But when they had tied him up with thongs, Paul said to the centurion who was standing by, "Is it legal for you to flog a Roman citizen who is uncondemned?" When the centurion heard that, he went to the tribune and said to him, "What are you about to do? This man is a Roman citizen." The tribune came and asked Paul, "Tell me, are you a Roman citizen?" And he said, "Yes." The tribune answered, "It cost me a large sum of money to get my citizenship." Paul said, "But I was born a citizen." Immediately those who were about to examine him drew back from him; and the tribune also was afraid, for he realized that Paul was a Roman citizen and that he had bound him.

Since he wanted to find out what Paul was being accused of by the Jews, the next day he released him and ordered the chief priests and the entire council to meet. He brought Paul down and had him stand before them. . . .

When the dissension became violent, the tribune, fearing that they would tear Paul to pieces, ordered the soldiers to go down, take him by force, and bring him into the barracks.

That night the Lord stood near him and said, "Keep up your courage! For just as you have testified for me in Jerusalem, so you must bear witness also in Rome." . . .

The Romans Escort Paul to Caesarea
Then he summoned two of the centurions and said, "Get ready to leave by nine o'clock tonight for Caesarea with two hundred soldiers, seventy horsemen, and two hundred spearmen. Also provide mounts for Paul to ride, and take him safely to Felix the governor."

Jesus prayed for God to have mercy on His attackers as He hung from the cross. Do Paul's actions in the first part of our reading reflect this same spirit of mercy? Why or why not?

In Exodus 19:5, God tells the Israelites that the whole earth belongs to Him. How do you see God's power over the kingdoms of the earth reflected in today's Scripture reading?

Paul was escorted from Jerusalem to Caesarea Maritima by 470 battle-hardened Roman soldiers. What do you think he was feeling when he walked from the barracks to find so many armed men waiting for him?

APPLICATION

The Roman army was one of the most powerful fighting forces ever assembled. They were known for their discipline, organization, and merciless efficiency. In Jerusalem, they were tasked with a particularly challenging mission: keeping the peace.

By the time Paul stood on the steps of the barracks, there had been multiple uprisings by the Jews in Jerusalem as they attempted to cast off their Roman occupiers. As a result, the soldiers stationed in the Antonia Fortress, which was adjacent to the temple, were quick to intervene if there was any hint of a disturbance.

When the Jews dragged Paul from the temple and began beating him to death in the middle of the street, the Roman commander was quick to respond. God used the Romans to both save Paul's life multiple times in quick succession and swiftly and securely move him on to the next phase of his mission.

Paul was strategic in planning his missionary journeys. The main cities he visited were important centers of power in the Roman world, an empire that had only recently begun deifying its emperor. When he arrived to preach the Gospel, he was sending the clear message that there is only one true King, and it isn't Caesar. Jesus the Messiah is Lord of all.

That is why he had longed to go to Rome, the center of the empire, for a long time.

As Paul was riding through the night to Caesarea Maritima, escorted by over four hundred Roman soldiers, there was no small sense of irony. God used the very oppressors the zealots hoped the Messiah would cast out of Israel to break the hold of the true enemy He had come to defeat, the forces of darkness.

The earth is the Lord's. All of it. He can, and will, use even the most unlikely, seemingly unfit, servants to accomplish His purposes. Paul was safe in the Roman's hands because they were held in the hands of an Almighty God.

Do you need God's deliverance today? Lift your eyes to the Father and wait in expectation for His rescue. You never know from which direction it may come.

thank you.

PROMPT

Describe a time when the most unlikely person was used by God in your life.

Take a moment to thank God for His protection and deliverance.

DIG DEEPER

Proverbs 21:1
Psalm 24:1–2
Romans 8:18–28

DAY 24

A Promise Long Delayed

Four walls. One ceiling. One floor. One door, locked tight.

This is Paul's world.

For two years, life has passed by on the other side of those four walls. Merchants haggle with customers in the marketplace as fishermen toss their nets into the Mediterranean Sea. Men and women fill the four thousand seats of the theater, watching as the actors take their places on the ornate stage. Ships sail into the manmade harbor with their wares, as women fill jugs with water from a spring miles away, carried into the city by an aqueduct for their convenience.

Not far from Paul's cell, Antonius Felix, the brutal, corrupt governor of the province, enjoys all the trappings of Herod the Great's seaside palace. He hosts banquets and fills the many ornate bedrooms with visiting dignitaries. He swims in the Olympic-sized pool and strolls through the garden. He lounges on the porches, drinking fine wine while enjoying the ocean breeze. He relaxes in the steamy waters of a Roman bath. He holds court, collects bribes, and fills his coffers with gold.

Paul just sits in his cell, marking time, waiting for life to begin again.

Before arriving in Caesarea Maritima, Paul spent years on the road, and hundreds of miles passed beneath his feet along the way. In cities all over the Roman world, he preached the Gospel, healed the sick, and freed the demon-possessed. He was stoned, thrown in prison, flogged in the synagogues, and brutally beaten in the streets. None of it stopped him. Tirelessly, relentlessly, he moved on from one city to the next, sharing the good news of Jesus the Messiah with anyone who would listen.

Now, when he was so close to making it to Rome, the heart of the empire, his world had come to a standstill.

When Paul was last in Jerusalem, Jesus appeared to him in a vision with the good news that he was, at last, headed to Rome. When he first arrived in Caesarea Maritima and was presented to Felix, that trip seemed imminent.

Then everything stalled. Felix made his excuses, locked Paul up, and seemed to forget about him entirely.

Days passed, and the wounds Paul suffered during the mob attack in Jerusalem slowly healed. Weeks passed as friends brought him supplies and tried to encourage him. Months passed as Paul worshiped and prayed. Years slipped by as he shared the Gospel with anyone who happened to pass the door of his cell.

For 739 days, Paul worshiped, witnessed, and prayed in a world comprised of four walls, one ceiling, one floor, and one locked door.

Waiting, waiting, waiting for Jesus to fulfill His promise to him, a promise long delayed.

SCRIPTURE READING

Read the Scripture below for the account of how Paul waited in custody for two years for Jesus to fulfill His promise to him.

Acts 23:34–35; 24:22–27 NRSV

Paul Presented to Felix
On reading the letter, [Felix] asked what province [Paul] belonged to, and when he learned that he was from Cilicia, he said, "I will give you a hearing when your accusers arrive." Then he ordered that he be kept under guard in Herod's headquarters.

After Paul's Hearing with His Accusers
But Felix, who was rather well informed about the Way, adjourned the hearing with the comment, "When Lysias the tribune comes down, I will decide your case." Then he ordered the centurion to keep him in custody, but to let him have some liberty and not to prevent any of his friends from taking care of his needs. . . .

Paul Held in Custody
Some days later when Felix came with his wife Drusilla, who was Jewish, he sent for Paul and heard him speak concerning faith in Christ Jesus. And as he discussed justice, self-control, and the coming judgment, Felix became frightened and said, "Go away for the present; when I have an opportunity, I will send for you." At the same time he hoped that money would be given him by Paul, and for that reason he used to send for him very often and converse with him.

After two years had passed, Felix was succeeded by Porcius Festus; and since he wanted to grant the Jews a favor, Felix left Paul in prison.

LET'S REVIEW

What is Felix waiting for when he first orders Paul to be held under guard?

While Festus was supposedly waiting for more evidence, he repeatedly called Paul to speak with him. Why did he do this?

While in Jerusalem, Jesus appeared to Paul in a vision to tell him that he was going to Rome, and at first, it seemed like everything was working out for that to happen. Instead, Paul was locked away under Roman guard for a very long time.

What struggles do you think Paul had during his wait? How do you think he felt while enduring this long delay with no idea when it might end?

APPLICATION

Paul once admonished the church in Rome to "rejoice in hope, be patient in suffering, persevere in prayer" (Romans 12:12 NRSV). He had many opportunities to live out his own teaching. His incarceration in Caesarea Maritima was surely one of those times.

How often must Paul have paced the perimeters of his cell in frustration? How many times did he remember the night Jesus appeared to him and wonder why that promise had not been fulfilled?

How did this man of ceaseless energy and relentless drive fill two years of long days and even longer nights waiting for the next phase of his life to begin?

Most certainly, Paul, who once challenged the church in Thessalonica to pray without ceasing, was in constant intercession for the churches under his care. He must have also prayed about his own circumstances as well, seeking God's face, during his long wait.

It is safe to assume that the same man who sang hymns while suffering in a Roman dungeon also filled his days of waiting with songs of praise. And if we have learned anything about Paul, he shared the Gospel every chance he got. Felix certainly seems to have gotten a much bigger dose of the Gospel than he ever wanted to hear.

Paul was stuck. It must have been discouraging and frustrating, but he didn't waste a moment of his wait.

There are times in our lives when we find ourselves languishing, wondering when God will answer our prayers or fulfill His promises to us. Those times are never easy, but we can follow Paul's example of enduring them patiently and faithfully.

We can pray. We can worship. We can point those nearest to us to the hope of Christ.

Are you waiting for God to move today? Keep your eyes expectantly on the Father. He will move again. You can trust Him, even when it seems His promises have been delayed.

hope of Christ

PROMPT

Think about a time when you found yourself waiting for God to fulfill His promises to you. Journal about what you learned during that season (or if you are in a season of waiting now, journal what you are learning today).

DIG DEEPER

II Peter 3:8–9
Psalm 13
I Corinthians 10:13

DAY 25

To the Emperor You Will Go

Paul shuffles along the luxurious hallways, with frescoes on the walls and intricate mosaics beneath his feet, his chains rattling. The sound of a fountain drifts through a window, carried along by salty sea breezes.

Soon, he arrives at the palace's audience hall. The guard swings open the heavy doors to reveal the new governor, Festus, seated on a platform ready to hear his case. A cluster of Jewish men from Jerusalem look up as he enters, their chins set in anger, their eyes hungry for vengeance.

The guard leads Paul to stand before Festus, and the men begin to make their charges against the apostle. When they finish, Paul has a chance to respond. He keeps it short and to the point: Their charges are untrue.

Festus listens to both sides, but his primary interest is not in justice but in scoring points with the Jewish leaders. The prisoner doesn't really have much to offer him. The Jewish leaders, however, are another story. It might be nice to have them in his debt. They want Paul transferred to Jerusalem because they are hoping to kill him along the way.

Perhaps Festus could arrange a change of venue. He offers Paul the "opportunity" to return to Jerusalem for trial.

Paul, however, knows better. He is under no illusions about what will happen if he makes that trip. He isn't afraid to die. He has been close to death so many times before, and he is ready to be with Jesus when the time comes.

But . . . he still has work he wants to accomplish. Jesus said he would go to Rome, and Paul has waited two years for that to happen. He isn't ready to die yet. He has one last card to play, and it is time to play it.

His Roman citizenship has served him well during his ministry. When he was last in Jerusalem, it not only spared him a flogging but also provided him with heavily armed guards to escort him safely out of the city. Now that citizenship would save his life once again, and in doing so, carry him to Rome at last.

Paul looked steadily into Festus's eyes and appealed his case to the highest court in the land, as was his right as a citizen. He wanted to appear before the emperor himself. It was a high-risk strategy. There was little hope that the emperor of Rome would grant a poor Jewish prisoner justice.

The emperor was a man of status. Paul was a prisoner.

The emperor was wealthy. Paul was poor.

The emperor had almost limitless power. Paul had none.

But Paul had something the emperor did not—he was filled with the awesome power of God.

Nearby, an oil lamp, fashioned from clay by a potter's hand, rested in its niche in the wall. If it were knocked to the ground, it would shatter into pieces. Useless, it would be swept up and thrown out into the street. The lamp wasn't very impressive on its own. It was a fragile vessel made of earth, but because of what was *inside it*, it gave light to the whole room.

"We have this treasure in clay jars," Paul wrote, "so that it may be made clear that this extraordinary power belongs to God and does not come from us" (II Corinthians 4:7 NRSV).

Paul was the clay pot, fragile and weak, but the power of God was alive and well within him, ready to spread the good news of the Gospel in Rome.

To the emperor he would go.

SCRIPTURE READING

Acts 25:1–12 NRSV

Three days after Festus had arrived in the province, he went up from Caesarea to Jerusalem where the chief priests and the leaders of the Jews gave him a report against Paul. They appealed to him and requested, as a favor to them against Paul, to have him transferred to Jerusalem. They were, in fact, planning an ambush to kill him along the way. Festus replied that Paul was being kept at Caesarea, and that he himself intended to go there shortly. "So," he said, "let those of you who have the authority come down with me, and if there is anything wrong about the man, let them accuse him."

After he had stayed among them not more than eight or ten days, he went down to Caesarea; the next day he took his seat on the tribunal and ordered Paul to be brought. When he arrived, the Jews who had gone down from Jerusalem surrounded him, bringing many serious charges against him, which they could not prove. Paul said in his defense, "I have in no way committed an offense against the law of the Jews, or against the temple, or against the emperor." But Festus, wishing to do the Jews a favor, asked Paul, "Do you wish to go up to Jerusalem and be tried there before me on these charges?" Paul said, "I am appealing to the emperor's tribunal; this is where I should be tried. I have done no wrong to the Jews, as you very well know. Now if I am in the wrong and have committed something for which I deserve to die, I am not trying to escape death; but if there is nothing to their charges against me, no one can turn me over to them. I appeal to the emperor." Then Festus, after he had conferred with his council, replied, "You have appealed to the emperor; to the emperor you will go."

LET'S REVIEW

Why does Festus ask Paul if he would like to go to Jerusalem for trial?

Paul was a man from two worlds. As a Pharisee, he was a conservative Jew, but he was also a Roman citizen by birth. In our Scripture today, how do you see these two identities come into play?

The Roman emperor was incredibly powerful. Paul, a Jewish prisoner without wealth or position, was not. What risks do you think Paul undertook by requesting an audience with the emperor?

APPLICATION

There are pottery shards all over Israel. They are mixed with the stones beneath your feet so thoroughly that it takes a trained eye to spot them. But once you see them, you can't unsee them. They are everywhere.

Until plastic arrived in Israel, pottery was a big part of everyday life in the form of plates, cups, oil lamps, and jars of every size. When a piece of pottery cracked, it was no longer of any use, so the owner would simply toss it out the door to shatter it, returning it to the earth from which it came. This happened a lot because clay jars are useful but are also very fragile.

Paul employs this image in his second letter to the Corinthians as he attempts to explain to them that the power at work in the Christian life is God's alone. We are simply the fragile vessels through which He chooses to pour His resurrection power into the world.

> But we have this treasure in clay jars, so that it may be made clear that this extraordinary power belongs to God and does not come from us. We are afflicted in every way, but not crushed; perplexed, but not driven to despair; persecuted, but not forsaken; struck down, but not destroyed; always carrying in the body the death of Jesus, so that the life of Jesus may also be made visible in our bodies. (II Corinthians 4:7–10 NRSV)

The Paul we met in the early days of our study was young, bold, and full of himself, but not anymore. He has been refined by suffering. He is humbler. His confidence in God's wisdom and power, however, has only grown stronger.

Now, as he begins to take the final steps of his journey, this transformation is on full display. After languishing in custody for two years under Felix, Paul now appears before the new provincial governor, Portius Festus, a man far more interested in furthering his political objectives than serving justice. Paul listens calmly as the Jews from Jerusalem, who clearly have no problem holding a grudge for two long years, make serious accusations against him.

Once again, Paul's life hangs in the balance.

A younger, brasher Paul might have lost his temper and lashed out, but this Paul sees the world and his place in it more clearly. He knows his position is fragile. He understands he has neither position nor power, but he also knows that the power of God remains within him, vibrant, unwavering, unstoppable.

So Paul the prisoner claims the rights of his Roman citizenship by appealing for his case to go directly to the highest power in the land—the emperor.

On the surface, this is a risky, foolhardy move. What hope does a poor Jewish prisoner have before the most powerful man in the Roman empire, a man whom many people worship as a god?

Paul, however, is unshakable. He might be as fragile as a clay pot, but he knows that he is filled with the incomparable power of God. He is confident that God's strength is made perfect in his weaknesses. The emperor might hold Paul's life in his hands, but God holds his eternity. What matters most to Paul is not whether he will survive his trip to Rome, but whether God's Word is carried to the ends of the earth.

This fragile clay pot, filled with the awesome power of God, will remain useful right up until the very end. His heart is steadfast, courageous, and at peace. To the emperor he will go.

Are you facing circumstances in your life that seem far beyond your ability to handle? That is okay. You can be fragile. You can be weak.

The awesome power of God is within you, and that is all you need.

PROMPT

What images come to mind as you consider today's reading? Journal about them.

DIG DEEPER

I Corinthians 2:1–5
II Corinthians 12:8–10
Matthew 10:16–20

DAY 26

Hope Goes on Trial

Flowing robes. The scent of perfume and spices. Gold and jewels glowing beneath the lamplight.

Festus takes his seat in front of the tribunal. King Agrippa II and his sister Bernice sit on either side of him. They have come to pay their respects to the new governor, and Festus senses an opportunity.

He doesn't exactly know what to do with the strange Jewish prisoner Felix left in his cell. The man turned out to have Roman citizenship and has appealed to the emperor. If Festus is going to send him to Rome, he knows he had better follow procedure. That means writing up an official account of the charges, and since his accusers' charges against him are weak at best, Festus is in a difficult position. Maybe Agrippa and Bernice can help.

Once everyone is in place, Festus calls for the prisoner.

Paul is led into the room by a guard to stand before Festus and his guests. Roman military officials wait nearby, red capes on their backs and swords on their belts, as the most influential and wealthy men of Caesarea watch Paul with curious eyes.

Paul, however, focuses his attention on the governor and his royal guests. Like Paul, Agrippa and Bernice, the great-grandchildren of Herod the Great, are from two different worlds. Although Jewish by birth, they were raised and educated in Rome. While Paul spent his childhood studying in the bet midrash and memorizing the Scriptures, Agrippa and Bernice sat in Roman schools undergoing a thorough indoctrination in the values and beliefs of the empire.

The room quiets, and Agrippa gives Paul permission to present his defense. Surrounded by royalty, powerful governmental officials, the wealthy, and the influential, Paul is determined to make the most of it.

He is on trial, he argues, because of *hope*.

Paul understands his Jewish accusers' hope well, because it was once his own. They hope in the Torah and the temple. They hope in a Messiah who, if only they can remain pure enough, will come at last to drive Rome from their land and set them free.

Agrippa and Bernice have placed their hope in Rome and all the power and privilege the empire offers them.

Paul, however, has a different hope. His hope is in the resurrection, the hope of a creation freed from the curse of death through the sacrifice of Jesus. Paul's hope isn't wishful thinking or optimism. In fact, it isn't a feeling at all. It is an expectation that God will remain faithful to His word.

It's a hope powerful enough to give him the courage to preach the Gospel before royalty and go to Rome to face the emperor. It's a hope sure enough to steady his soul even when the storms rage and the night is dark.

It's a living hope, a hope that will carry him to the ends of the earth in service of a risen Savior. And when his work is finished, hope will carry him home.

SCRIPTURE READING

Acts 25:23–26:23 NRSV

So on the next day Agrippa and Bernice came with great pomp, and they entered the audience hall with the military tribunes and the prominent men of the city. Then Festus gave the order and Paul was brought in."

Agrippa said to Paul, "You have permission to speak for yourself." Then Paul stretched out his hand and began to defend himself:

"I consider myself fortunate that it is before you, King Agrippa, I am to make my defense today against all the accusations of the Jews*, because you are especially familiar with all the customs and controversies of the Jews; therefore I beg of you to listen to me patiently.

"All the Jews know my way of life from my youth, a life spent from the beginning among my own people and in Jerusalem. They have known for a long time, if they are willing to testify, that I have belonged to the strictest sect of our religion and lived as a Pharisee. And now I stand here on trial on account of my hope in the promise made by God to our ancestors, a promise that our twelve tribes hope to attain, as they earnestly worship day and night. It is for this hope, your Excellency, that I am accused by Jews! Why is it thought incredible by any of you that God raises the dead?

"Indeed, I myself was convinced that I ought to do many things against the name of Jesus of Nazareth. And that is what I did in Jerusalem; with authority received from the chief priests, I not only locked up many of the saints in prison, but I also cast my vote against them when they were being condemned to death. By punishing them often in all the synagogues I tried to force them to blaspheme; and since I was so furiously enraged at them, I pursued them even to foreign cities.

"With this in mind, I was travelling to Damascus with the authority and commission of the chief priests, when at midday along the road, your Excellency, I saw a light from heaven, brighter than the sun, shining around me and my companions. When we had all fallen to the ground, I heard a voice saying to me in the Hebrew language, 'Saul, Saul, why are you persecuting me? It hurts you to kick against the goads.' I asked, 'Who are you, Lord?' The Lord answered, 'I am Jesus whom you are persecuting. But get up and stand on your feet; for I have appeared to you for this purpose, to appoint you to serve and testify to the things in which you have seen Me and to those in which I will appear to you. I will rescue you from your people and from the Gentiles—to whom I am sending you to open their eyes so that they may turn from darkness to light and from the power of Satan to God, so that they may receive forgiveness of sins and a place among those who are sanctified by faith in Me.'

"After that, King Agrippa, I was not disobedient to the heavenly vision, but declared first to those in Damascus, then in Jerusalem and throughout the countryside of Judea, and also to the Gentiles, that they should repent and turn to God and do deeds consistent with repentance. For this reason the Jews seized me in the temple and tried to kill me. To this day I have had help from God, and so I stand here, testifying to both small and great, saying nothing but what the prophets and Moses said would take place: that the Messiah must suffer, and that, by being the first to rise from the dead, He would proclaim light both to our people and to the Gentiles."

* Whenever we see the term "the Jews" in the New Testament, it means "Jewish leaders." Early Christianity was a sect of Judaism that believed Jesus was the Messiah. It was "Jewish Christianity." Paul never walked away from his Jewishness.

LET'S REVIEW

Herod Agrippa II and his sister Bernice were Herod the Great's great-grandchildren. These Jewish siblings were raised and educated in Rome. The first verse of our reading today gives us hints that they had assimilated to Roman culture. What does it say about how they entered the court? Who accompanied them?

The Jewish leaders made all sorts of accusations against Paul, but why did Paul say he is on trial?

As Paul testified, he recounted meeting Jesus on the road to Damascus. Why did Jesus say He was sending Paul to the Gentiles?

APPLICATION

When Paul is called to testify before Herod Agrippa II and his sister Bernice, he does so from a place of extreme vulnerability. He has just spent two years languishing in prison only to emerge to find that the same Jewish leaders who were scheming to take his life when he fled Jerusalem remain committed to the task. If he survives their plot, he will go to Rome to stand trial before the emperor, and his life will hang in the balance once again.

Somehow, under such extreme duress, Paul has the courage and clarity to shift the focus of the trial from the plots of the Jews and the politics of Rome to *hope*.

A careful reading of today's Scripture reveals that each of the individuals and groups represented have placed their hope in something.

Herod Agrippa II and Bernice were Jews who had completely absorbed Roman culture. We see them enter the tribunal with "great pomp," accompanied by representatives of the Roman military and some of the prominent citizens of Caesarea Maritima. There is historical evidence that points to a strong possibility that Agrippa and Bernice were more than brother and sister, that they lived as husband and wife, an inconceivable moral violation for Jews. Their hope was in Rome and the wealth and power it afforded them.

Paul's Jewish accusers have their own hope, one he quickly points out that he once shared. Their hope is that if they are careful enough to obey God's law, He will intervene and send a Messiah to run their Roman occupiers out of the country.

Paul, however, has a different hope. Like his accusers, he believes Moses and the prophets, but he has realized that everything they were teaching and prophesying pointed not to a Messiah who was a military hero, but to a Messiah who would deliver all creation from the curse of sin through His own suffering, death, and resurrection. The hope Paul demonstrates here is not a feeling; it is an *expectation* that the resurrection power of Jesus will ultimately prevail.

This type of hope is a determination to anchor ourselves into the bedrock of God's promises no matter what we see, no matter how great our fear, no matter how dark the night has fallen.

In his letter to the Romans, Paul writes, "I consider that the sufferings of this present time are not worth comparing with the glory about to be revealed to us. . . . For in hope we were saved. Now hope that is seen is not hope. For who hopes for what is seen? But if we hope for what we do not see, we wait for it with patience" (Romans 8:18, 24–25 NRSV).

Hope isn't a feeling. It is an act of defiance against death and despair rooted firmly in the promises of God.

Do you need hope today? Take hold of God's promises, claim them as your own, and never let them go. His Word never fails.

PROMPT

When you are in times of trial, what Scripture gives you hope? Take time to meditate on this passage today and journal about it.

DIG DEEPER

II Corinthians 3:7–18
Romans 8:18–24
Romans 5:1–11

DAY 27

Shipwrecked

The roar of the wind is deafening. Day turns to night, and night to day, as the ship carrying 275 souls is driven by the tempest. Up the sides of waves as tall as mountains, the small vessel climbs, only to rush headlong to the base of the wave on the other side.

Paul was on his way to be tried by the emperor. Sailors, soldiers, prisoners, and slaves become equals before the gale, each man simply hoping to make it out alive. They watch the sky, hoping for some sign that the storm will break, but there is no sun. No stars. There is only wind, rain, and the churning sea.

The sailors toss their precious cargo overboard to lighten the vessel. When that isn't enough, they throw their tackle over too. The ship creaks and groans.

The storm rages on, and all hope of survival is abandoned.

On the fourteenth night, the sailors realize they are nearing land. To slow the ship's approach, they toss an anchor overboard. It catches, and the ship lurches, straining against the tether. When it seems the rope will break, they cut it loose and toss a second anchor. They repeat the process four times, and when there is nothing else to try, they pray for daylight.

When morning nears, Paul shouts over the wind to get everyone's attention. He begins with an "I told you so," and then moves on to some good news. He has received a vision from God that though the ship will be lost, every man will survive. He encourages them to eat something, grabs a piece of bread for himself, and thanks God for it as the astonished passengers look on.

But when he begins eating, they follow his example, and for the first time in days, they dare to hope.

As the sun rises, the outline of a shore gradually takes shape in the gloom. The sailors spot a beach and turn the ship in that direction, planning to run it ashore. Each man watches as land grows nearer and nearer.

Then, with a terrible crash, the ship hits a reef. For the first time in two weeks, they are still. The bow is stuck fast, unmovable. The wind, however, rages on, furiously driving the waves against the battered vessel. The ship screams and groans like a living being fighting for its life.

Then it begins to break apart.

Those who can swim jump overboard and head toward land. Everyone else grabs whatever they can find that will float and leaps into the churning sea.

One by one, they crawl up onto the shore and collapse onto the sand.

Every man is saved. Sailors, soldiers, prisoners, and slaves are all equally indebted to the God of the wind and the waves.

SCRIPTURE READING

Read the passage below for the exciting account of how God saved Paul and everyone with him from a shipwreck.

Acts 27:13–44

When a moderate south wind began to blow, they thought they could achieve their purpose; so they weighed anchor and began to sail past Crete, close to the shore. But soon a violent wind, called the northeaster, rushed down from Crete. Since the ship was caught and could not be turned head-on into the wind, we gave way to it and were driven. By running under the lee of a small island called Cauda we were scarcely able to get the ship's boat under control. After hoisting it up they took measures to undergird the ship; then, fearing that they would run on the Syrtis, they lowered the sea anchor and so were driven. We were being pounded by the storm so violently that on the next day they began to throw the cargo overboard, and on the third day with their own hands they threw the ship's tackle overboard. When neither sun nor stars appeared for many days, and no small tempest raged, all hope of our being saved was at last abandoned.

Since they had been without food for a long time, Paul then stood up among them and said, "Men, you should have listened to me and not have set sail from Crete and thereby avoided this damage and loss. I urge you now to keep up your courage, for there will be no loss of life among you, but only of the ship. For last night there stood by me an angel of the God to whom I belong and whom I worship, and he said, 'Do not be afraid, Paul; you must stand before the emperor; and indeed, God has granted safety to all those who are sailing with you.' So keep up your courage, men, for I have faith in God that it will be exactly as I have been told. But we will have to run aground on some island."

When the fourteenth night had come, as we were drifting across the sea of Adria, about midnight the sailors suspected that they were nearing land. So they took soundings and found twenty fathoms; a little farther on they took soundings again and found fifteen fathoms. Fearing that we might run on the rocks, they let down four anchors from the stern and prayed for day to come. But when the sailors tried to escape from the ship and had lowered the boat into the sea, on the pretext of putting out anchors from the bow, Paul said to the centurion and the soldiers, "Unless these men stay in the ship, you cannot be saved." Then the soldiers cut away the ropes of the boat and set it adrift.

Just before daybreak, Paul urged all of them to take some food, saying, "Today is the fourteenth day that you have been in suspense and remaining without food, having eaten nothing. Therefore I urge you to take some food, for it will help you survive; for none of you will lose a hair from your heads." After he had said this, he took bread; and giving thanks to God in the presence of all, he broke it and began to eat. Then all of them were encouraged and took food for themselves. (We were in all two hundred seventy-six persons in the ship.) After they had satisfied their hunger, they lightened the ship by throwing the wheat into the sea.

In the morning they did not recognize the land, but they noticed a bay with a beach, on which they planned to run the ship ashore, if they could. So they cast off the anchors and left them in the sea. At the same time they loosened the ropes that tied the steering oars; then hoisting the foresail to the wind, they made for the beach. But striking a reef, they ran the ship aground; the bow stuck and remained immovable, but the stern was being broken up by the force of the waves. The soldiers' plan was to kill the prisoners, so that none might swim away and escape; but the centurion, wishing to save Paul, kept them from carrying out their plan. He ordered those who could swim to jump overboard first and make for the land, and the rest to follow, some on planks and others on pieces of the ship. And so it was that all were brought safely to land.

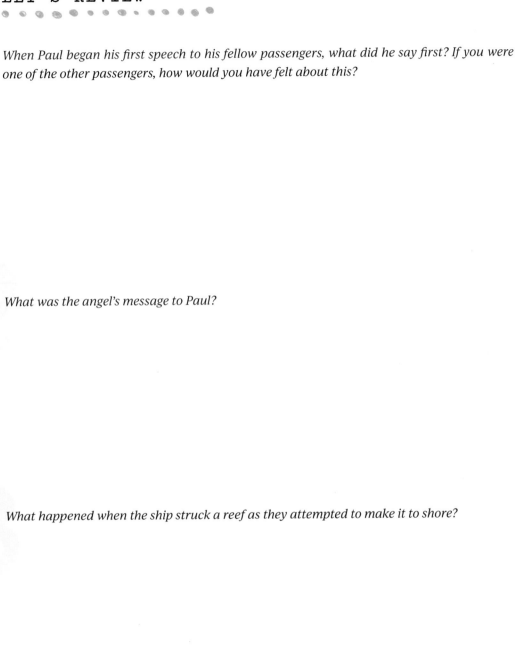

LET'S REVIEW

When Paul began his first speech to his fellow passengers, what did he say first? If you were one of the other passengers, how would you have felt about this?

What was the angel's message to Paul?

What happened when the ship struck a reef as they attempted to make it to shore?

APPLICATION

In today's lesson, we find a detailed account of the shipwreck that Paul, along with 275 other passengers, suffered on his way to stand trial before the emperor in Rome. For fourteen days, the ship is driven mercilessly by a storm so violent that they see "neither sun nor stars for many days" (Acts 27:20 NRSV).

The seasoned sailors find the circumstances so dire that they throw their valuable cargo overboard to lighten the vessel. A little while later, they toss the ship's tackle after it. When even these drastic measures fail to improve their situation, they give up all hope of making it out alive.

The ancient Israelites were not seafaring people. To them, the sea was a terrifying place. Once you understand this about their culture, so many passages in the Bible take on a new meaning.

When the psalmist writes of God mastering the sea, the very representation of danger and chaos, it is a metaphor for how the mighty power of God is able to save us from whatever overwhelms us and threatens to sweep us away. Psalm 65:7 proclaims,

> You silence the roaring of the seas,
>
> the roaring of their waves,
>
> the tumult of the peoples. (NRSV)

We see this imagery in Exodus as well. When the children of Israel find themselves with Pharoah's army behind them and the Red Sea before them, God miraculously intervenes and parts the water. Once they are safely on the other side, He allows the sea to return to its place, sweeping Pharoah's army away with it.

It is interesting to compare God's deliverance of the children of Israel at the Red Sea with His deliverance of Paul and his fellow shipmates. In both accounts, a group of people are in grave peril from the sea. In both accounts, God provides miraculous deliverance.

The difference is that, in the Exodus account, God saves only His people. In the case of Paul's shipwreck, however, God brings every single man to safety. Jews and Romans. Prisoners and soldiers. Sailors and passengers. Freedmen and slaves.

All are rescued.

This is a beautiful picture of what Paul had traveled the world to proclaim. Because of Jesus' death and resurrection, salvation is available to *everyone.*

But God isn't just the Savior of our souls; He is also Lord over the storms that terrify and overwhelm us as we navigate this broken world. He is both so mighty that He is the Redeemer of all creation and so tender that He invites us to turn to Him for shelter when all around us gives way.

Perhaps you find yourself in the middle of a storm today. You, like the sailors, may have done everything you can think of to find a solution to no avail. Day and night, you hear the wind howl and the boards creak beneath your feet.

Rest in this hope: Your God is Lord over the raging tempest. The wind and the waves, no matter how violent, are helpless before Him.

Your loving Savior is mighty to save.

PROMPT

Have you experienced a season of overwhelming turmoil that, like a raging storm at sea, threatened to sweep you away? Write a note to God below and thank Him for your deliverance. If the storm still rages for you, write a note to Him about your current circumstances.

DIG DEEPER

Psalm 107:23–31
Psalm 65:6–8
Psalm 89:8–9

DAY 28

Unlikely Provision

Dazed and weary, the men scan the coastline. They have survived the sea, but how will they survive a shipwreck on an island in winter when all their provisions lie at the bottom of the Mediterranean Sea?

They are soaked through, and the cold rain falling banishes any possibility of that changing anytime soon.

Then, in the distance, they see people running to them from the hillside above. When they arrive on the beach, they tell the castaways that they are on the island of Malta. The people had witnessed their shipwreck and have come to help.

Starting a fire for the cold and wet men is the first item on the agenda. Soon, they have a cheerful blaze going, and the castaways scatter to find wood to throw onto the fire.

Paul reaches down to toss his armload of sticks into the blaze. At that very moment, a venomous serpent leaps out of the flames and latches onto his hand.

Instinctively, he shakes it off into the fire. The natives know that Paul has just received a death sentence. As far as they are concerned, a man who survives a shipwreck only to immediately be bitten by a venomous snake must be under a curse from the gods. There is no saving Paul from this. The only thing left to do is to wait for the venom to do its work.

But it doesn't. The swelling never comes. His breathing stays steady, his heartbeat strong. When they realize he has suffered no ill effects at all from the bite, they change their minds and decide that he must be a god himself.

Perhaps this is what opens the door for all that comes next. A man named Publius, who owns land nearby, offers his hospitality to Paul and the others. They stay with him for three days, and during that time, they learn that Publius's father is terribly sick. Paul, moved with compassion and filled with the Holy Spirit, heals the man.

When word gets out about the miracle, the citizens of Malta bring others to Paul for healing too.

God uses it all to grant Paul favor. He and his companions find provision and safe shelter on the island throughout the winter. When spring arrives, and a ship is made available for them to continue onto Rome, the citizens of Malta even stock them with provisions for the journey.

God is faithful to make all things—even a shipwreck and a snakebite—work together for our good.

SCRIPTURE READING

Read the passage below to discover how God used the most unlikely circumstances to provide for Paul and his fellow castaways on the island of Malta.

Acts 28:1–10 NRSV

After we had reached safety, we then learned that the island was called Malta. The natives showed us unusual kindness. Since it had begun to rain and was cold, they kindled a fire and welcomed all of us around it. Paul had gathered a bundle of brushwood and was putting it on the fire, when a viper, driven out by the heat, fastened itself on his hand. When the natives saw the creature hanging from his hand, they said to one another, "This man must be a murderer; though he has escaped from the sea, justice has not allowed him to live." He, however, shook off the creature into the fire and suffered no harm. They were expecting him to swell up or drop dead, but after they had waited a long time and saw that nothing unusual had happened to him, they changed their minds and began to say that he was a god.

Now in the neighborhood of that place were lands belonging to the leading man of the island, named Publius, who received us and entertained us hospitably for three days. It so happened that the father of Publius lay sick in bed with fever and dysentery. Paul visited him and cured him by praying and putting his hands on him. After this happened, the rest of the people on the island who had diseases also came and were cured. They bestowed many honors on us, and when we were about to sail, they put on board all the provisions we needed.

When a snake bites Paul, what do the natives initially think it means? What about after he recovers?

What doors for ministry did God open after Paul survived the snakebite?

How do Paul and his friends obtain the necessary supplies they need to survive, as well as passage to Rome?

APPLICATION

Followers of Jesus often love to quote Paul's words in Romans 8:28 during times of trial: "We know that all things work together for good for those who love God, who are called according to His purpose" (NRSV).

Most of us, however, would much rather God provide protection from suffering in the first place. Who doesn't want "good" without pain?

In today's lesson, Paul had the opportunity to live out his words to the Romans. After surviving fourteen days in a terrible storm at sea, he was shipwrecked and survived! When he and his traveling companions crawled up onto the shore, they were met by the island natives, who rushed down to offer what help they could.

Paul, cold, wet, and certainly exhausted, must have felt such relief to draw near the fire they built. He even gathered some driftwood himself to toss into the blaze.

Only to have a venomous snake leap from the flames and latch onto his hand.

We don't know what Paul thought in that moment, but it is a safe guess to assume it was something along the lines of "You have *got* to be kidding me!"

His circumstances were so unfortunate that the natives assumed he was under some special punishment from the gods and his death was imminent. When God intervened and spared Paul's life, the natives decided that he was actually a god himself!

Perhaps it was this demonstration of power that opened the door for Paul to begin healing their sick and, of course, preach the Gospel as he did.

A shipwreck. A snake bite. What strange tools for God to use to bring healing and freedom to the residents of Malta and provide for Paul and his companions along the way!

Paul and his fellow castaways were stranded on a strange island with nothing to eat and no options for moving on to Rome. God, however, doesn't need favorable circumstances to provide for His children. He is quite happy to use the worst life throws at us and turn it around for our blessing, and that's exactly what He did for Paul on Malta.

The natives were so overwhelmed by the demonstration of God's power through Paul that they sheltered and fed the entire group of 276 castaways over the winter. When spring came and a ship became available, the citizens of Malta even provided provisions for the journey.

It is incredibly difficult to keep fear at bay in times of crisis and suffering. The wind howls, the waves churn, and everything we were counting on to carry us safely to shore falls apart beneath us. Then, just when it seems we might make it, a new set of troubles comes our way. Even the most faithful among us find ourselves wondering what on earth God is up to in a moment like this.

But that is often when God shows up and shows off the most. He takes the very thing that was threatening to destroy us and somehow, miraculously, turns it around.

Is the storm raging around you today? Does it feel like you have been hit with one heartbreak after another until you can no longer see a way out? Place your need in the Father's hands. He may be working at this very moment to turn your trials into blessings.

PROMPT

What images come to mind when you imagine God turning your trials into blessings? Journal about it.

DIG DEEPER

Philippians 4:19–20
Matthew 6:25–34
II Corinthians 9:6–10

DAY 29

Making the Most of Every Opportunity

Paul and the Roman solider assigned to guard him made their way through the busy streets of Rome as Luke followed behind them. Merchants haggled with customers in the ground-floor shops of the many insulae, the multistory "apartment" buildings where all but the wealthy Romans lived, as the sounds of daily life drifted from the large open windows of the apartments on the upper floors.

The men slowed to a stop in front of the insula in which Paul, who was responsible for his own expenses, had rented an apartment. After a moment, they ducked into the dark stairwell, Paul's chains rattling as they began their climb.

Soon, they opened the door to the apartment the three men would call home until they received the summons to appear in court. The room was dark, the only light slipping in from the edges of the heavy cloth hanging over the large window facing the street. Occasionally, a gust of cold wind blew the cloth inward, allowing the meager winter sunlight to briefly pierce the gloom.

Their accommodations were sparse. The insulae were connected to neither the aqueducts, even though they reached the shops on the bottom floor, nor the sewer system. This meant they had to acquire their own water from the public fountains and use chamber pots, disposing of the contents by throwing them unceremoniously into the street below.

The apartment's furnishings included a few oil lamps, sleeping mats, and a bronze brazier, which held coals for cooking. The warmth of a woodburning stove, like those back home in Judea, would have been welcome, but it was impossible. Not only was there no way to vent the smoke, but flames larger than those held within the brazier were forbidden due to the risk of fire. Daily life in Rome afforded the men few comforts.

Paul was a prisoner on house arrest, awaiting trial before Caesar, the most important man in the Roman world, but he was determined not to waste his wait.

Since he was unable to go to the synagogue to share the Gospel, as was his custom in each city he visited, he invited the local Jews to come to him. They filled his small home and listened all day as he proclaimed the arrival of Jesus the Messiah. Some of them believed, but many others didn't. His heart was broken as he watched them leave.

Would they ever really listen? It was the same struggle he had faced in every city on his journeys. As he had done each time before, he now turned to the Gentiles.

For two years, Paul waited for his trial, but he used every moment to share the good news about Jesus. He preached boldly, ceaselessly, to anyone who would listen.

Paul was shackled with chains, but the Gospel remained unbound.

SCRIPTURE READING

Read the Scripture below to learn how Paul made the most of his time while incarcerated in Rome.

Acts 28:16–31 NRSV

When we came into Rome, Paul was allowed to live by himself, with the soldier who was guarding him.

Three days later he called together the local leaders of the Jews. When they had assembled, he said to them, "Brothers, though I had done nothing against our people or the customs of our ancestors, yet I was arrested in Jerusalem and handed over to the Romans. When they had examined me, the Romans wanted to release me, because there was no reason for the death penalty in my case. But when the Jews objected, I was compelled to appeal to the emperor—even though I had no charge to bring against my nation. For this reason therefore I have asked to see you and speak with you, since it is for the sake of the hope of Israel that I am bound with this chain." They replied, "We have received no letters from Judea about you, and none of the brothers coming here has reported or spoken anything evil about you. But we would like to hear from you what you think, for with regard to this sect we know that everywhere it is spoken against."

After they had set a day to meet with him, they came to him at his lodgings in great numbers. From morning until evening he explained the matter to them, testifying to the kingdom of God and trying to convince them about Jesus both from the law of Moses and from the prophets. Some were convinced by what he had said, while others refused to believe. So they disagreed with each other; and as they were leaving, Paul made one further statement: "The Holy Spirit was right in saying to your ancestors through the prophet Isaiah,

'Go to this people and say,
You will indeed listen, but never understand,
    and you will indeed look, but never perceive.
For this people's heart has grown dull,
    and their ears are hard of hearing,
        and they have shut their eyes;
        so that they might not look with their eyes,
    and listen with their ears,
    and understand with their heart and turn—
        and I would heal them.'

Let it be known to you then that this salvation of God has been sent to the Gentiles; they will listen."

He lived there two whole years at his own expense and welcomed all who came to him, proclaiming the kingdom of God and teaching about the Lord Jesus Christ with all boldness and without hindrance.

LET'S REVIEW

When Paul was in Rome awaiting trial before Caesar, he wasn't in prison. What were the circumstances of his confinement?

Whenever Paul arrived in a city on his missionary journeys, he always began preaching in the synagogue. Because of his circumstances in Rome, how did he meet with and teach the Jews there?

How long was Paul confined in Rome? How did he occupy himself during that time?

APPLICATION

Jeremiah 29:4–7 is a fascinating passage of Scripture in which God gives instructions to the Jews who were ripped from their homes and taken into exile by the Babylonians. Without a doubt, these families were hoping for one message from God—an announcement that He was getting them out of there and returning them to Israel!

Instead, God tells them to settle in, build houses, plant gardens, and grow their families. In short, God tells them to bloom where they are planted!

Our Scripture reading today finds Paul on a two-year house arrest in Rome while awaiting trial before Caesar. We might expect this hiatus to show up as a blank space in Luke's account. After all, what could Paul really accomplish while under guard?

As it turns out, quite a lot.

We are given a detailed account of how, when he was unable to go to the synagogue to share the Gospel, he called the Jews to come see *him*. Once he had spent a day sharing the good news of Jesus with them (with mixed success), he moved on to the Gentiles.

Luke tells us that Paul spent the next two years sharing the Gospel with anyone who came to him "with all boldness and without hinderance" (Acts 28:31 NRSV).

When we are faced with deeply disappointing circumstances, it's easy to feel like all our options have been expended, all doors closed. Paul shows us in today's reading that there is always some way we can love and serve others.

In Ephesians 5:8–16, Paul challenges his readers to make "the most of every opportunity, because the days are evil" (NIV). Our time on this earth is limited, so bloom where you are planted.

Love God. Love your neighbor.

Make the most of every opportunity.

PROMPT

Take some time in prayer to ask God to show you whom to share His love with today. Write down your plan, then come back later and record your experience.

DIG DEEPER

Ephesians 5:8–16
Jeremiah 29:4–7
I Corinthians 10:31

DAY 30

I Have Fought the Good Fight

Paul is in prison in Rome, and the end is near. He picks up a scroll and a pen and writes to Timothy, the young man who had become more than a student, more than a fellow missionary. Timothy was, in many ways, like a son.

I am being poured out like a drink offering. . . .

The pen hovers over the scroll for a moment as Paul gathers his thoughts. Goodbyes are always hard, but like any good father facing his death, he has things he wants to say to this young man who holds such a special place in his heart.

Paul has escaped death so many times. He has been beaten, flogged, imprisoned, shipwrecked, and even stoned. Each time, God has restored him so that he might press on, carrying the Gospel to the end of the world.

And that he has done.

This time, though, he feels deep in his spirit that things will turn out differently. His work is finished, and although it breaks his heart to leave those he loves, he is ready to see Jesus face-to-face.

His pen drops to the scroll again.

The time for my departure has come. . . .

Departure, not death. For if there is one thing Paul believes with all his heart, it is that he will live again. Because of Jesus, the crucified Messiah who rose again, death has been defeated!

Long hours in his cell, with little to do other than think, have Paul looking back over his life since the day Jesus met him on the road to Damascus and gave him the mission to carry the Gospel to the Gentiles. With deep satisfaction, Paul knows he has been faithful.

He dips the pen in ink and lowers it to the scroll again.

I have fought the good fight, I have finished the race, I have kept the faith.

But Paul is tired. His soul is weary, worn, and marked by the grief that inevitably accompanies great love. There were times, when he needed comfort the most, that it felt like everyone he trusted walked away. He forgave them, of course, but it still hurt.

He takes a deep breath, then writes on.

At my first defense no one came to my support, but all deserted me. May it not be counted against them! But the Lord stood by me and gave me strength. . . .

But the Lord.

What a beautiful interruption in the narrative! Yes, Jesus has always been faithful. On the days when Paul found himself at the end of his resources, so weary that he couldn't imagine taking another step, Jesus gave him strength. No matter what suffering came his way, Emmanuel, the God who is with us, never left his side. Still, Paul's chains are heavy. His body, which has suffered so much abuse, aches.

Paul has served. He has loved. He has taken the good news of Jesus the Messiah to the ends of the earth. Now he is determined that he will continue to praise the Messiah right up until he draws his final breath.

The Lord will rescue me from every evil attack and save me for His heavenly kingdom. To Him be the glory forever and ever. Amen.

Paul's work is done. Heaven is calling.

Emmanuel is forever near.

SCRIPTURE READING

Read Paul's poignant letter to Timothy in which he reflects on a life lived in faithful service to God.

II Timothy 4:6–18 NIV

For I am already being poured out like a drink offering, and the time for my departure is near. I have fought the good fight, I have finished the race, I have kept the faith. Now there is in store for me the crown of righteousness, which the Lord, the righteous Judge, will award to me on that day—and not only to me, but also to all who have longed for His appearing.

Do your best to come to me quickly, for Demas, because he loved this world, has deserted me and has gone to Thessalonica. Crescens has gone to Galatia, and Titus to Dalmatia. Only Luke is with me. Get Mark and bring him with you, because he is helpful to me in my ministry. I sent Tychicus to Ephesus. When you come, bring the cloak that I left with Carpus at Troas, and my scrolls, especially the parchments.

Alexander the metalworker did me a great deal of harm. The Lord will repay him for what he has done. You too should be on your guard against him, because he strongly opposed our message.

At my first defense, no one came to my support, but everyone deserted me. May it not be held against them. But the Lord stood at my side and gave me strength, so that through me the message might be fully proclaimed and all the Gentiles might hear it. And I was delivered from the lion's mouth. The Lord will rescue me from every evil attack and will bring me safely to His heavenly kingdom. To Him be glory for ever and ever. Amen.

LET'S REVIEW

The winner of the Isthmian Games, which were held near Corinth, received a crown woven from dried celery. What type of crown does Paul say he expects to receive from the Lord?

What does Paul say about the Lord's presence in his life when people abandoned him in his time of need?

Considering Paul's circumstances, it would be understandable if he felt God had let him down. In the final portion of our Scripture reading, how does he respond instead?

APPLICATION

After giving us a riveting account of Paul's life from the moment in which he oversaw the stoning of Stephen to his arrival in Rome to appear before Caesar for trial, Luke, the author of Acts, puts down his pen without finishing the story.

When we last see Paul, he is under house arrest while waiting for his trial. We don't know what happened when he stood before Caesar. There is no recording of his testimony or whether he was exonerated or condemned.

Paul's second letter to Timothy, however, gives us some hints. He mentions his "chain" and arriving in Rome. So it seems that Paul is in prison in Rome, and this time, he doesn't expect to make it out alive.

His letter is reflective and poignant, a beautiful expression of his faith and who he was as a man. As Paul writes to Timothy, he looks back over his life and ministry, evaluating his service to Jesus, and he is confident in what he finds. He has been faithful to his calling. He has served well.

The letter carries with it a shadow of sorrow as Paul ponders his suffering, made more painful by his abandonment by trusted friends. Beneath the grief, however, is a strong undercurrent of joy found in the faithfulness of Jesus.

"The Lord stood by me," he writes (II Timothy 4:16 NRSV).

In John 16:33, Jesus warned His disciples that they would have trouble in this world, and anyone who has walked this earth knows that to be true. As the creation awaits its ultimate renewal when Jesus returns, the forces of evil continue to cause chaos and destruction. Paul knew this better than anyone. He suffered deeply throughout his ministry, and it seems likely that his life ended in suffering.

His hope, however, is ours as well. No matter how devastating our circumstances, we never walk alone. When those we trust abandon us in our hour of need, Jesus remains close. He bends His ear low to hear our prayers and bears witness to every tear.

He is Emmanuel, God is with us, and nothing can separate us from His love.

> Who will separate us from the love of Christ? Will hardship, or distress, or persecution, or famine, or nakedness, or peril, or sword? As it is written,
>
> "For Your sake we are being killed all day long;
>
> > we are accounted as sheep to be slaughtered."
>
> No, in all these things we are more than conquerors through Him who loved us. For I am convinced that neither death, nor life, nor angels, nor rulers, nor things present, nor things to come, nor powers, nor height, nor depth, nor anything else in all creation, will be able to separate us from the love of God in Christ Jesus our Lord. (Romans 8:35–39 NRSV)

PROMPT

Ponder what you have learned in this study. Which lesson was most influential for you? Journal about it.

DIG DEEPER

II Corinthians 9:24–27
Matthew 1:18–24
Deuteronomy 31:1–8

ABOUT THE AUTHOR

SHANNA NOEL *is the founder and owner of Illustrated Faith and the Bible-journaling community. Her other well-known devotional journals include* 100 Days of Bible Promises, 100 Days of Grace and Gratitude, *and* 100 Days of Less Hustle, More Jesus. *Shanna lives in the Pacific Northwest with her husband of twenty years, Jonathan, and their two daughters. When they aren't doing something creative as a family, you can find them playing a board game with a bowl of fresh popcorn and lots of laughs.*

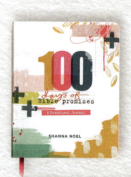

ABOUT THE AUTHOR

SHERRI GRAGG *utilizes cultural background, and her unique style of storytelling, to immerse readers in some of the most riveting moments in Scripture. She is the author of five books including* Advent: The Story of Christmas *(Dayspring, 2019) and* Arms Open Wide: A Call to Linger in the Savior's Presence *(Thomas Nelson, 2016). Sherri is a nationally published freelance writer and mother of five children. She lives and writes in beautiful Franklin, Tennessee.*

For more from author Sherri Gragg, check out *Advent: The Story of Christmas.*

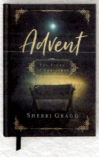

Available at **dayspring.com**

as well as several retail stores near you.

Dear Friend,

This Bible resource was prayerfully crafted with you in mind—it was thoughtfully written, designed, and packaged to encourage you right where you are. At DaySpring Bibles, our vision is to see every person experience the life-changing message of God's love, not just on Sundays, but every day of the week. As we worked through rough drafts, design changes, edits and details, we prayed for you to encounter His unfailing love and indescribable peace within the pages of this book. It is our hope that this resource doesn't only fill your head with knowledge, but strengthens your connection with and understanding of God.

THE DAYSPRING BIBLE TEAM

Additional copies of this book and
other DaySpring titles can be purchased
at fine retailers everywhere.
Order online at dayspring.com
or
by phone at 1-877-751-4347

From Where I Stand: 30 Days in the Life of Paul
Copyright © 2022 Shanna Noel, all rights reserved.
First Edition, October 2022

Published by:

21154 Highway 16 East
Siloam Springs, AR 72761
dayspring.com

Cover Design, Artwork and Concept by: Shanna Noel
Written by: Sherri Gragg
Sherri Gragg is represented by Lisa Stilwell at Loadstone Literary. See LoadstoneLiterary.com.

Printed in China
Prime: J7570
ISBN: 978-1-64870-440-6